"A really useful toolkit for up-and-coming managers"

—**Vincent Cobee, ex-CEO of Citroen**

"Practical and compelling"

—**Sam Eads, Head of Ad Sales, Trainline**

HOW TO BE MODERATELY SUCCESSFUL

Career Acceleration for Realists

MATTHIAS MAHR

How To Be Moderately Successful.

Copyright © 2025 by Matthias Mahr.

All rights reserved. No part of this book may be reproduced or transmitted in any form or by any means without the written permission of the author.

ISBN: 978-1-0682184-7-7 (Paperback)

Cover and interior design by CoverKitchen.

It matters not how strait the gate,
How charged with punishments the scroll,
I am the master of my fate:
I am the captain of my soul.

—WILLIAM ERNEST HENLEY,
INVICTUS

"Forty-two," said Deep Thought,
with infinite majesty and calm.

—DOUGLAS ADAMS,
THE HITCHHIKER'S GUIDE TO THE GALAXY

Contents

Introduction: Why 'moderate success'? 11

PART 1
HOW TO UNDERSTAND YOURSELF 15

What even is success? 16

Your 5-minute personality tests: Are you a Fiery Red ENTP? 20

A Brief Interlude: It's all your fault 28

Your personal brand: Are you IKEA or Apple? 30

No, you're not the only one who can't sleep at night 37

PART 2
HOW TO BE GOOD AT YOUR JOB (THE BASICS) 43

Aiming high: "Ça, c'est du vrai insight" at BCG Paris 44

Managing expectations: Your easyJet flight is delayed 47

Keeping focus: The exam question 53

Managing time: Trying to avoid 'al desko' 57

A Brief Interlude on being honest 65

Sending emails: Don't be a Boov 68

Writing presentations: Avoiding 'death by PowerPoint'... 71

Being proactive: "Einer geht sich immer noch aus" 79

Moving on from setbacks: The 5 stages of grief 84

Finding balance: The Stockdale Paradox 89

PART 3
HOW TO WORK WITH OTHER PEOPLE 95

Understanding people (1): What they do 97

Working with third parties 106

Understanding people (2): Who they are 112

Showing humility: Three men go camping 119

A Brief Interlude on swearing 123

Understanding people (3): Where they're from 125

Managing your boss 138

Making people feel special: Free fries in Greece 144

Working with idiots 149

Active listening: An endangered skill worth honing 156

PART 4
HOW TO BE GOOD AT YOUR JOB (ADVANCED) **161**

Strategy is deciding what not to do 163

Setting goals: Aboard the riverboat *Steam Queen*........... 169

Solving problems: The hypothesis-based approach 174

Making decisions: You don't always need to 'sleep on it' 180

A Brief Interlude on humour 186

Negotiating well (1): Why cinemas
only sell giant tubs of popcorn 189

Negotiating well (2): Getting my teenagers out of bed .. 194

Setting prices: Restaurant 97 in Surbiton 199

Managing people and projects: Let it go, let it go! 204

Reinventing things: Never waste a good crisis 210

PART 5
HOW TO GET A BETTER JOB **217**

Defining your 'value proposition' 219

Developing your career: Get a mentor, or two 223

Getting promoted (1): Know the process(es) 228

Getting promoted (2): Step up! 235

A Brief Interlude on luck 239

Fantastic jobs and where to find them 241

Working with headhunters: It's not you, it's them 250

A Brief Interlude on job titles 255

Impressing people at interviews: My top ten tips 257

Succeeding in a new role: How hard can it be? 264

Epilogue: To moderate success, and beyond! 269

Acknowledgements 271

Further reading 275

About the author 276

Introduction: Why 'moderate success'?

This isn't your usual business book. It doesn't take its lessons from famous people, doesn't promise to make you rich and won't make you a world expert on anything. Instead, it takes as a starting point what it's really like to work in a typical job in a typical corporate environment, facing into this reality and *accelerating it* — all the while maintaining a healthy work-life balance.

Think of *moderate success* as your Everest base camp and this book as your mountain guide — full of shortcuts and local knowledge, but also realistic about the tough trek ahead. From there, you can absolutely push on and climb all the way to the summit. Or if you prefer, you can just enjoy the view down into the valley with a cold drink in hand, watching others struggle on ahead — how *you* ultimately define success is up to you and indeed that's where we'll start our journey.

This is a self-help book for people who are ambitious, but realistic. For people who want to learn, but don't have the patience for complicated theories. For people who want to be coached, not lectured. For people who like to have a bit of fun along with the serious. For people who want to take action.

And why would you trust me to be your guide to *moderate success*? Because I speak from experience across multiple countries in a variety of successful — and sometimes less successful — roles, while building a life outside of work. (Hi friends and family! Thanks for all your help.) Because the contents of this book have been patiently accumulating in my phone's notepad for years, waiting to see the light of day when the time was right. And because I genuinely want you to progress, just like the many direct reports, peers, junior and senior employees from all departments, who seemed to enjoy the coaching conversations we had (with some reminding me years later).

The book's short chapters are organised in a broadly logical order under five headings: Understanding Yourself, Being Good At Your Job (Basic and Advanced), Understanding Others and Getting Promoted, but you're welcome to dip in and out as you see fit or jump straight to an area that feels particularly relevant and come back to the rest later. In each chapter, you'll find an exercise so you can put your learnings into practice straight away. These are always clearly highlighted and I've left you enough space to write your answers into the book — that way, you start accumulating a bank of knowledge and can remind yourself later on if needed.

And now, get your hiking boots on. It's time to start the climb!

PART 1

HOW TO UNDERSTAND YOURSELF

If you're like me, you'll want to dive into the actions straight away. "Tell me what I can do to improve", I hear you say, "after all, that's what you promised me on the back cover"! Fair enough and fear not, there'll be plenty of opportunities coming very soon.

However, having a good understanding of yourself — what drives you, who you want to be and most importantly, what you want to achieve, is the fundamental basis of achieving moderate success. After all, if you don't know what you're trying to achieve, how do you know if you've achieved it?

In fact, this first part is so important that I'd encourage you not only to complete the chapters but also share the findings with close family or friends, to get their feedback. So before you get started, have a think about whom you might bring into your circle of trust. It'll be worth it.

And with that, let's get going. I hope you have fun.

What even is success?

In the past, the answer to this question may have been relatively straightforward and involved a big job in a well-known company, a nice house and car, and perhaps some worthy role in the local community.

How times have changed. Nowadays, and rightly so, we're all allowed, nay encouraged to define success on our own terms rather than having it imposed on us from the outside. Well, most of the time anyway. I'm 48 as I write this and my dad still asks me occasionally when I'll finally get a real job that he can boast to all his friends about. And I had a CEO recently tell me that when they were between roles, they purposefully gave themselves 9 months off so that their father-in-law wouldn't keep asking why they were still unemployed.

Putting any nagging relatives to one side for a minute, before we start it's really important that you're clear on what success means for you. While we might not get to a beautifully crisp answer with a bow on top, at least you should have an outline in mind that you can work towards. So let me ask you a few questions that will hopefully help.

Question 1: What sort of time frame are you thinking about?
At one end of the spectrum, you could frame it as 'what can I look back on when I'm retired?' or at the other end, 'where will I be in six months'? Have a think about what's best for

you. As a default, I'd probably recommend a three to five year time horizon because it'll be long enough to make a real difference but not so long that you lose sight of the here and now. Plus, who knows what's going to happen in ten years' time. But ultimately, it's your personal decision.

Question 2: What's the point of it all?
No, not life in general (although 'why are we here' is a tremendously interesting question) but why are you seeking professional success? Is it to prove something to yourself, your friends, your family? Is it to feel fulfilled so that you've 'done something with your life'? Is it to feel powerful? Or is it really just for the money, so you can do more fun things in life? You may not have a definite answer but at least having that discussion with yourself (or better, with someone close to you) will help get some clarity on your goals.

Question 3: How important is professional success in the context of the rest of your life?
Of course, we'd like to have it all but I'd encourage you to be realistic here and accept that you can only *fully* commit to two of the following three things at any one time: Work, family and hobbies. Start with family as you might not have much of an option there, especially if you have small children — in which case you're left with a choice of work or hobbies as your 'second major'. Now that my kids are older, I do have a little more freedom but as a keen runner, it still means that I can only train hard if I'm either out of work or accept to spend less time with my family. So have a good long think, how important is professional success for you? And by extension, what trade-offs are you willing to make? This is not

a trick question. All answers are valid here including 'I want to work as hard as I can to move up as fast as I can' or 'I'm happy to take it a bit easier as long as I can finish a marathon and still spend time with my kids'. Clearly, to some extent it's a question of balance but being clear about your own priorities here is really important.

Question 4: Whom do you admire and aspire to be like?
To make it more tangible, it's helpful to have an aspirational benchmark of someone who looks like they've had the sort of success that you're aiming for. You can create a composite persona of multiple people here if you'd like and in some ways that's probably better — in case your one chosen person turns out to be less impressive than they first appeared! By all means give yourself a stretch target, although remember that you're aiming for moderate success, so I would advise against picking the Beckhams or Taylor Swift. In fact, I'd recommend picking only non-celebrities so that it all becomes a bit more real.

ACTION

Based on your answers above, write down the best expression of what success means to you. This is hard and it doesn't have to be perfect, but have a go at something like this: 'By age X, I'd like to have progressed to a role such as Y while also achieving Z outside of work.' As you go through the rest of the book, it'll be helpful to occasionally refer back to this objective to make sure you stay focused on the prize. If you want, you could put a framed version above your desk for easy reference (and motivation), but that bit is optional.

Your 5-minute personality tests[1]: Are you a Fiery Red ENTP?

Now that you've defined your ultimate objective, let's move on to understanding how you operate in a professional context: In order to figure out your path, not only do you need to know the destination but also how your strengths and weaknesses may influence your journey. For this, I'm going to suggest two personality tests to give you an indication of your dominant traits and preferences, so you can adjust your focus accordingly.

I was initially a little sceptical — perhaps even cynical — about the value of these tests, but I'll happily admit that there's always a modicum of truth in the findings even if you're tempted to game the answers. I've certainly learned a lot about myself from the many tests I've had the chance to complete over the years, including the fact that I have a 'dark side' trait of being occasionally mischievous!

I'd therefore encourage you to grab any opportunity to take such tests if they're offered (typically as part of interviews, development or team-building) — indeed, you might have already completed some. They generally involve assessing a very long list of statements, some sillier than others,

---

1 Not a trick to lure you in: Actually 5 minutes

such as 'I enjoy breaking rules' (well yes, I do occasionally) or perhaps 'would you rather be a dog or a cat' (has to be cat). Eventually, you'll be classified along a number of axes and/or typecast into a certain bucket, as well as given a detailed description of your way of operating.

As a convenient shortcut, here are radically simplified versions of two of the most common personality tests for you to either discover or refresh. Take them with a pinch of salt, but I'm confident that they'll give you a good directional understanding of your preferences and remember that there are no right or wrong answers!

MYERS-BRIGGS (MBTI)®

The OG personality test, first devised by Katharine Myers and Isabel Briggs in the 1940s. While it's no longer quite *du jour*, it's a good starting point so please answer these four questions as best you can:

Q1: *After a couple of hours at a busy drinks reception, do you feel tired or invigorated?*
Tired > You are an I for Introvert
Invigorated > You are an E for Extrovert

Q2: *If someone comes to you with a 'big idea', are you generally more excited about the opportunity or more concerned about the feasibility?*
Excited > You are an N for iNtuition[2]
Concerned > You are an S for Sensing

---

2 Yes, you'd think they could have found a word starting with the letter N (or picked a different letter)

Q3: Do you make decisions primarily with your head or your heart?
Head > You are a T for Thinking
Heart > You are an F for Feeling

Q4: When you wake up on Saturday morning, do you already have a plan for the weekend?
Yes > You are a J for Judgment
No > You are a P for Perception

Voilà! If you put your four letters together (for example, mine is INTJ), you have your MBTI® profile. You can add a bit of nuance by considering how easy you found it to answer each question — for example, I am a 'strong' T and J, but a 'weak' I and N. Of course, on its own your profile isn't very helpful, but later in this chapter we'll focus on what to do with this information. In the meantime, I'd recommend spending a few minutes searching up your profile online for a detailed description.

INSIGHTS DISCOVERY® 'COLOUR WHEEL'

Probably because there are four not sixteen possible outcomes, this seems to have become the default personality test recently, so much so that interviewers' eyes normally light up when I say that I'm a reasonably balanced profile of Red mixed with some Blue and a little Yellow.

There's a good chance that you already know what colour you are, but you may wish to use this section to remind yourself. In essence, this test uses the 'Introvert vs Extrovert' and 'Thinking vs Feeling' axes to create a 2x2 matrix, with each quadrant assigned a colour as shown.

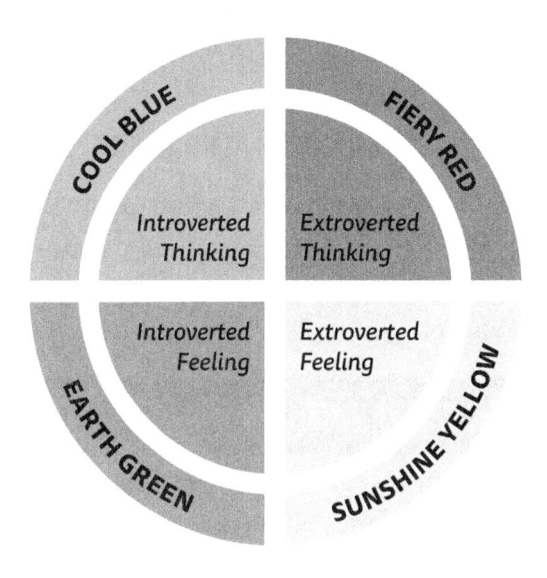

A diagram shows a circle divided into four quadrants labeled:
- **Cool Blue** (top-left): Introverted Thinking
- **Fiery Red** (top-right): Extroverted Thinking
- **Earth Green** (bottom-left): Introverted Feeling
- **Sunshine Yellow** (bottom-right): Extroverted Feeling

To pick your colour, you can use your answers from the first test, perhaps double checking them against these summary descriptions:

- **Fiery Red:** You're energetic and strong-willed (some might say pushy)
- **Cool Blue:** You're organised and analytical (some might say over-precise)
- **Sunshine Yellow:** You're sociable and enthusiastic (some might say excessively bubbly)
- **Earth Green:** You're caring and supportive (some might say soft)

As before, the outcome isn't as quite as simple as a single colour and it's possible — though not required — for your profile to be split between different colours, with one more or less dominant, such as mine described above. Once again, if you search online for the different colours you'll get a lot more detailed information.

OTHER PERSONALITY TESTS

There are plenty of other personality tests out there, including Hogan (showing both your 'bright side' and — intriguingly — your 'dark side') and Belbin (focusing on team roles). If you're interested, you can find more information online.

ACTION 1

Write down your two profiles here so you don't forget. Also, can you add a short description of your 'dark side', i.e. what less desirable trait you start showing when you're under pressure?

WHAT TO DO WITH THIS INFORMATION

Ultimately, knowing your preferences increases your self-awareness, which in turn allows you to build on your strengths, address your blind spots, and improve your interactions with others, particularly if their preferences are different.

Let's first look at your profiles in isolation. Your existing preferences will mean that you'll find certain parts of your work harder than others — strong Is may hate team meetings, for example, while strong Ps may find it difficult to get things finished. While you shouldn't aim to change who you are (because it's futile and because it's what makes you unique), you do need to ensure that you balance out any very strong preferences.

Using myself as an example, both my 'T' and my 'J' are very strong, which can mean not sufficiently taking into account people's feelings and not reacting well to last-minute changes. Over the years, I've developed some workarounds to make sure I don't appear cold-hearted and inflexible, such as reminding myself not only to look at the numbers and taking my time before commenting on a change of plan. Be careful how you implement any changes, however: I once worked with an introvert senior leader who wanted to appear more approachable but found it difficult, so every Friday he walked the office floor using a bowl of fruit as an ice-breaker. It was very awkward.

The second, possibly more important, application is how your profile interacts with that of others. If you and a colleague both have similar traits, it's much more likely that you'll get on well because it'll just feel natural. On the other hand, if your traits are the opposite, let's say Red and Green or INTJ and ESFP, you might initially think that you're talking to an alien! We'll come back to understanding other people in Section 3, but you can already try and increase your awareness of those differences today, to avoid any unnecessary issues.

As you go through the book, pay particular attention to those chapters that feel more uncomfortable or further away from your normal preferences: one of my objectives is to leave you with a more rounded profile overall, so nothing holds you back.

ACTION 2

Based on your profile answers, write a short action plan of the key axes that you'd like develop further, and how you might go about it. Perhaps have a look at the table of contents and identify any chapters that might be particularly useful.

A Brief Interlude: It's all your fault

Before we continue, I need you to promise me something: That you'll stop complaining about how in certain situations the world is against you and if it hadn't been for x, y or z you'd already be way further ahead in your career. Yes, I'm sure that you've been desperately unlucky at times and your boss may well be an idiot. And I know that it feels great to whinge about it or that occasionally you can't avoid having a day where you think that nothing will ever go right.

But a really important lesson of this book is that everything that's happened in your career is your fault. Well, of course it's not directly your fault but it indirectly is, because it (almost) all happened as a consequence of decisions you made. I'm not saying that at the time you could have made better ones (although I certainly could have), but what I am saying is that the only person who can change your trajectory is *you*.

I realise that this may seem a bit rich coming from a white, male writer who's been fortunate enough to have a reasonably sheltered upbringing and a good education. We all come from very different backgrounds and I'm not denying that some of us get a significant head start. Nonetheless, now that you're in the working world you need to take charge and any disadvantage you may have had will get smaller over time.

A BRIEF INTERLUDE: IT'S ALL YOUR FAULT

Incidentally one of the first business books I ever read was 'The Seven Habits of Highly Effective People' by Stephen Covey[3]. He's sold over 25 million of them so you can pick up a cheap copy second-hand, but it's not my kind of read because it takes 420 pages to explain seven ideas so I recommend Wikipedia for a free summary instead. The book did however have one lasting effect on me, which is its first habit: Be Proactive. In practice this means that only you can determine your fate by trying to actively influence it. Not all of your attempts will work, but at the end of the day you need to be in charge of your own destiny — control the things that you can control, as the saying goes.

So bear this in mind when going through the book and particularly when completing the actions. You can be successful, I'm sure of it, but you need to work at it and make the changes that are required to get there. I hope this book will serve as your inspiration and perhaps, offer you a wake-up call.

---

[3] See Further Reading.

Your personal brand: Are you IKEA or Apple?

In business, a valuable brand is a crucial element of success for many companies, particularly those selling to consumers. And by valuable I don't just mean familiarity with its name and logo (although of course that helps), but also affinity with its values and beliefs, some of which will have been built up over decades. Brands like IKEA or Apple have a head start over competitors because customers already know what they stand for, even if they don't always agree.

What makes up a brand? There are as many definitions out there as there are people working in marketing, but for the purpose of this exercise I'd like to focus on what I call the 'brand pyramid'. This often includes an overall brand promise (= the brand in a nutshell), supported by the emotional and rational benefits of the brand (= what customers will get) and then the reasons to believe (= the factual evidence supporting those claims). To illustrate, I have reproduced here an example I created for eBay, the online marketplace, back in 2008[4].

---

[4] I didn't ask eBay for permission to reproduce this, but as it's my own work and almost 20 years old I hope that I can keep the eBay lawyers at bay. Only time will tell.

Pyramid Diagram

BRAND PROMISE: Shopping worth talking about

EMOTIONAL BENEFITS: I'm **excited** by the find / I'm **proud** to be a savvy shopper

RATIONAL BENEFITS: The right deals for me
- I can find exactly what I want
- I can get great deals
- I can discover items I didn't know existed

REASONS TO BELIEVE: World's biggest, most varied selection
- Variety and multitude of sellers
- Fresh inventory every day
- Unique and established marketplace structure

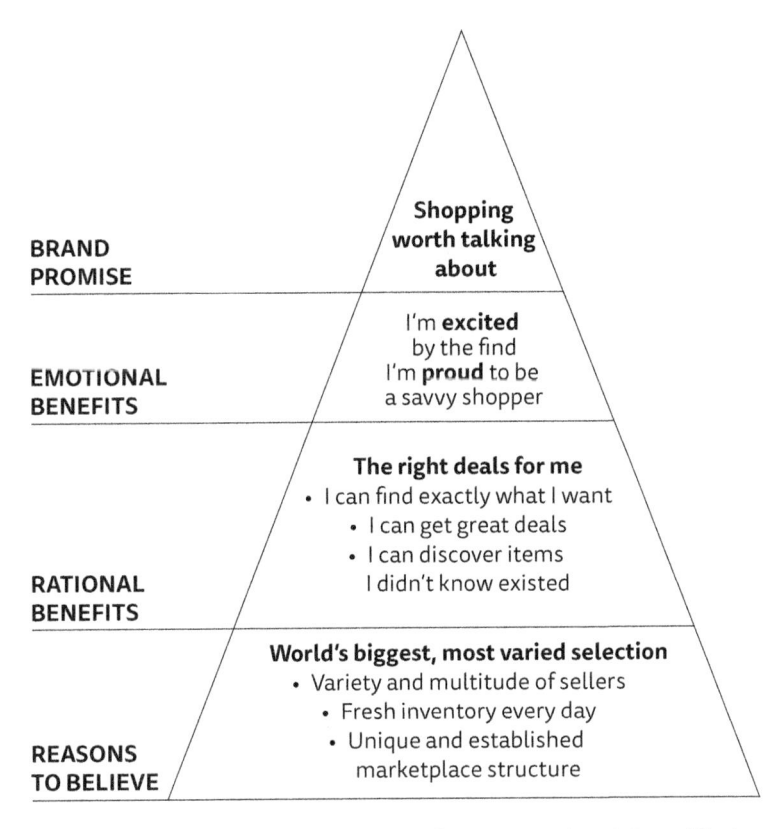

You may ask why I tell you about this, given that it's unlikely that you'll be able to affect your company's brand identity and this section is about understanding yourself, not your company. That's because people are mini-brands just as much as companies are maxi ones.

That's right: You may not have recognised it yet but you, yes you, are just as much a brand as Amazon, Apple and Facebook. Your audience might be a little smaller than theirs, but the same principle applies: Define your personal brand and work to perfect it, and you will reap the rewards. If you think I've gone mad, you need only look at the most successful businesspeople, politicians or entertainers and you can see it jumping out at you: Oprah Winfrey, the friendly guide through your tricky life; Roger Federer, the suave gentleman; Taylor Swift, the uber-entertainer and best friend of teenage girls; and on it goes. You might not like all of these people, but you can't deny that everyone knows who they are and what they represent, making further success much easier to achieve (and lucrative endorsements much easier to source).

But personal brands aren't just for famous people. Being clear on the definition and consistent in the execution can help everyone stand out from the crowd and therefore become *moderately successful* more quickly — particularly so in large organisations where it may be difficult to get your head above the parapet. Don't expect quick wins, however. Just like company brands, personal brands take time to build and perfect but will pay off in the long run.

Let's have a go at defining your own personal brand, focusing initially only on the brand promise at the top, which should be a pithy summary of what makes you unique. Ideally this is something that'll hold true forever, but if in doubt, aim for where you'd like this to be in future rather than where it is today.

But how to do it? As a shorthand, you could just pick an existing brand as an analogy, say cars (posh Ferrari or reliable Volvo?), technology (design-led Apple or edgier Samsung?) or indeed the uber-efficient IKEA. Or pick a famous person or perhaps an animal (cheetah or meerkat) that you'd like to emulate. If you find that too simplistic (or weird), then instead answer the following questions:

- In a work context, what makes you stand out from other people?
- How would your co-workers describe you?
- Why should a company hire you rather than someone else with similar experience?

Some of the dominant personality traits we discussed in the previous chapter may also flow into your personal brand. As an example, my brand promise is: 'Reliably excellent delivery, with a glint in my eye', meaning that you can always trust me to do my work really well, but I'm also fun to have around and will push the boundaries a bit. (As an aside, in an ideal world, your personal brand would also be valid in your personal life, rather than simply being a work persona — but I accept that some people prefer to act differently in work and personal contexts, so start with work and branch out from there.)

ACTION 1

Using the questions above, write down your 'brand promise' in ten words or fewer (any more and it'll be too complicated). Don't aim for perfection, because you're not going to stick a print-out on the office wall, but do aim for clarity and be honest with yourself.

This exercise is hard and you can refine it later if you wish, but at least you have a starting point. I hope it's also given you a mini-lift as it's nice to know that you've got a special touch, right? And if you haven't managed to write anything down, chat to your friends and family to get some inspiration. Everyone is unique in some ways — yes, that includes you — so it's just a question of finding out.

The next step is to put your personal brand into practice. This isn't about standing on a soap box[5] in the office shouting 'look at me, I deliver results', but about nudging people's perceptions through lived experience every day.

---

5   Actually, there is one soap box that you do need to stand on, and that's your LinkedIn profile. Once you're done with this chapter I'd recommend making sure that it reflects your personal brand, as does your CV.

ACTION 2

Now focus on the 'reasons to believe' your brand promise. Draw two columns and complete them with 1) three concrete examples where you've demonstrated your brand promise very well and 2) three examples where you haven't. Going forward, aim to move the examples in column two to column one.

By the way, company brands are not limited to the expression of the brand pyramid but normally also include a recognisable visual identity (including the logo plus colours, fonts and imagery) and a unique tone of voice (normally expressed as a series of words, for example 'natural, elegant and engaging' at an upmarket hotel company). If you enjoyed the exercises above, you *could* go there and also adapt the way you look and speak to the personal brand you've defined, but that might be going a bit far so is entirely optional.

Indeed as with all things in life, there is a balance to be struck. Keep quiet about what makes you unique and you'll just be a face in the crowd. Flaunt your wares too ostentatiously and it might come across as a bit strange. But small changes will add up over time and it's worth the effort — better be slightly quirky and talked about than beige and unknown.

No, you're not the only one who can't sleep at night

Before we move onto tips and tricks for doing a good job, we have to talk about one of the big Elephants In The Room: Stress, and how to deal with it.

I've been a 'stress pot' for as long as I can remember: I'll always find something to worry about and once one concern has gone away then another will take its place — work related or otherwise. And let's be clear about one thing: A little bit of stress is good for you, because it keeps you on your toes and can act as a useful catalyst to get things done.

However, in a recent role the stress got seriously out of hand, as I was juggling too many responsibilities while trying to hit very stretchy targets. For a while, I couldn't figure out a solution so struggled to fall (and stay) asleep and had a few days where I could barely contemplate coming into work. It was not a sustainable place to be and I needed to sort it out.

For most ambitious people, the stress balance will occasionally tip too far into the red and you'll find yourself in a situation where you're starting to worry that you can no longer cope. There are many ways in which this can manifest, from nervous tics to a lack of concentration to irritability, and most annoyingly for many people the inability to sleep: you either can't fall asleep or wake up in the proverbial 'pool of sweat' much earlier than you would have wanted, leading to tiredness which can quickly build up.

If a version of this is happening to you then let me share some thoughts that might help. First of all, a quote by American tennis legend Billie Jean King, which is inscribed on a plaque mounted at the entrance to the US Open Centre Court: *Pressure is a privilege*. I know it's trite and when you're properly stressed out, I doubt you're feeling particularly privileged, but if someone's giving you a lot of pressure then implicitly it means that this person believes in you, and that's likely because you're good at what you do. So to some extent, take it as a compliment.

The second and more important point is that you're not alone in feeling stressed or sleeping badly from time to time. Except that because it's quite personal and to many people, a little embarrassing, you don't talk about your sleep issues to your colleagues, even the ones you trust the most, so you think you're the only one. Particularly at 3am when it's dark and you're lonely and the world feels like a really tough place. (Having a cat can help with the night-time loneliness, mine while a little confused is delighted to see me on my occasional nocturnal visits.)

Please take some comfort from the fact that for almost everyone, the world is occasionally a tough place and life is occasionally really hard and they are also having trouble sleeping. They're just not telling you about it, just like you're not telling them! This is certainly what I found when I started opening up to a few chosen friends and colleagues. Their answer was invariably a version of "oh yes, that happens to me all the time".

So what can you do about excessive stress? Here are some recommendations for you to consider based on my own experience:

- Accept that some stress is part of life, that some days are worse than others, and that everyone survives a couple of uncomfortable nights

- Explore the power of breathing and meditation. I tried a couple of mindfulness apps, but I just didn't have the patience for their overly soothing voices (oh, the irony!) and found they stressed me out more rather than less. However, I've found breathing exercises before going to sleep very helpful, so I'm sure there's something out there for you too

- Consider writing down your concerns so they don't continuously circle in your head

- And of course, if your current job is a key driver of your high stress levels, then you need to find a way to address that. Try and reduce the key sources of stress or if that isn't possible, consider changing roles as a last resort

- Most importantly, talk to someone about it, so you have a partner in crime. This can be your friend or partner, or if you think it may be helpful, a professional stress counsellor

Of course stress, including its manifestations and how to deal with them, is an incredibly complex subject and I'm not saying that the above will solve all of your issues. But just remember this: we're all in the same boat, so don't try rowing all on your own.

> **ACTION**
>
> Find a trusted friend with a reasonably similar job to yours. Ask them how they deal with stress, particularly when it gets really bad. You might have to ask two or three people, but I'm convinced that you'll find someone to sympathise with very quickly.

PART 2

HOW TO BE GOOD AT YOUR JOB (THE BASICS)

Now that you've found out a little bit about yourself, we can really get started on the work-related actions. We'll begin with the basics of doing well in any job — setting expectations, managing your time and effort, communicating your ideas clearly, and dealing with the ups and downs of working life.

Depending on your experience, you may already be quite familiar with some of these topics, but I'm sure there are some though-provoking ideas for everyone, not least in the chapter about being honest! Let's get started with setting the right bar, and we'll take it from there.

Aiming high: "Ça, c'est du vrai insight" at BCG Paris

After my first job as a consultant in London in the late nineties, I was lucky enough to go off and do an MBA in the United States. I learnt a lot but despite explicitly taking a course on self-understanding, I really wasn't any the wiser about the job I wanted afterwards. So the safe thing to do, especially given the dotcom bubble of the early 2000s, was to go back into consulting, except that this time it would be with a better-known firm (Boston Consulting Group or BCG) and in Paris rather than London.

I arrived in Paris in September 2002 thinking that this gig would be easy. After all, I'd already done three years as a consultant, spoke decent French (having learnt it at school) and am an optimist at heart, so what could possibly go wrong?

It turned out that working at BCG in Paris was nothing like working at MMG (my previous company) in London, for two reasons. One, the French working environment was a lot less fun than that in London — for a start, the whole workspace was split up into actual offices shared by two consultants each and the concept of beers after work didn't really exist. In fact, it took me a good three months to be invited out for my first social occasion so I had a rude transition from *Work Hard, Play Hard* in London to *Work Harder, Don't Play Much* in Paris. Sunday afternoon walks through the Île Saint-Louis partly made up for this, but it was a lot less enjoyable than I expected.

However, the expected quality of work was, I'm happy to admit, a lot higher than it had been in London. They weren't just aiming high, they were aiming very high. This was often a reasonably painful experience as presentations were written, re-written and then re-written again regardless of the time invested or indeed the time of day. It was certainly the only job where I ever had a full team meeting scheduled at 1am, because the senior people genuinely cared about getting to a great answer. They did not however care very much about the work life balance of their people, so dinners and weekend trips were regularly postponed at the last minute, and *fun* it was not.

While I'm not sure I necessarily want to repeat the experience, it's certainly stuck with me since then as it's taught me to aim high, or as a different company used to call it, *raise the bar*. So before we go into specific tips and tricks, I'd like to instil in you a simple yet profound desire not to settle for mediocre work and to keep pushing the envelope. Is your output really as good as you think? When was the last time you delivered something that was truly excellent? Are you asking the uncomfortable questions that will get to the best answers?

I'm not saying that every piece of work you'll do from now on will be truly revolutionary, with people at your feet for its sheer brilliance. I also recognise that aiming high is a lot easier when you're surrounded by others doing the same and all you need to do is ride the wave. But to achieve your goals, I'd like you to try — just as I was told to do at BCG Paris until eventually the Partner would stroke their (often imaginary) beard, smile softly and exclaim: "Oui. Ça, c'est du *vrai* insight[6]". And I'd smile back, tired but deeply content.

> **ACTION**
>
> Write down the name of someone whose ability to consistently raise the bar for performance inspires you. Keep them in mind as a sort of North Star next time you deliver a piece of work and ask yourself: Would they have been satisfied with the level of quality?

---

6   Yes. That is real insight.

Managing expectations: Your easyJet flight is delayed

Imagine you're sat on an aeroplane that's about to depart. You're feeling anxious as you have dinner plans with friends upon arrival. Then, the captain's voice echoes over the speakers: "I'm sorry, there's a small delay before we can leave as we're waiting for clearance and it's quite busy. It shouldn't take too long." You're feeling quite positive as you boarded early so if all your transportation stars align, you'll still be on time. Now that would be a major result.

Unfortunately, 20 minutes later you're still sitting there. You're starting to get slightly annoyed but are still holding out hope for your dinner, if only you could push back in the next few minutes. The captain comes on again and says: "It shouldn't be much longer now, thanks for waiting."

You watch minute after minute ticking away and start thinking that to make the main course, you'll really need a favourable tailwind now. Another 20 minutes pass, at which point the captain says: "Sorry about the continued delay. We should receive clearance to leave very shortly now." By the time you actually leave another 20 minutes later, you're resigned to the fact that joining for dessert is the best you can hope for.

What will you tell your friends when you arrive? Probably something like "I really thought I'd make it, but then the delay just got longer and longer! It was really frustrating."

Now imagine you're sat on the very same aeroplane but right at the beginning, the captain comes on and says: "Sorry everyone, it looks like we'll be an hour late because of air traffic control delays". How would you feel? Really annoyed about your dinner, right? But you're probably going to readjust your expectations to just about making dessert, while by the time you eventually arrive only 30 minutes late you're feeling reasonably good about sneaking that main course after all. So what will you tell your friends then? Maybe something like "I was lucky the delay wasn't as long as expected — I didn't think I was going to be here this early".

In both scenarios, the plane's arrival time was exactly the same, but in the second example, you're likely to feel much better about it. That's because your expectations were set suitably low so that the eventual result was *better than you thought*. In the first example, expectations were high and the reality progressively worsened, so not only was it *worse than you thought*, you were disappointed multiple times in a row.

A pithier way to express this is:

Satisfaction = Performance - Expectations.

Can you see where this is leading in a work context? Your performance at work doesn't exist in a vacuum and will always be compared to a benchmark of sorts, so the formula above tells you that there are *two* ways of increasing satisfaction: The obvious one, increasing performance (i.e., doing better work) and the less obvious one, decreasing expectations. In other words, underpromise and overdeliver.

A word of warning: If you're not careful, this can be a slippery slope towards mediocrity, with lower expectations driving lower performance. So let me be clear: *Aiming High* is still key, just as the easyJet pilot was doing everything they could to speed up departure. However, managing expectations is an important part of how your work is perceived and must therefore be part of your toolkit.

The prime application of this principle is at your company's goal setting time, typically a quarterly or annual process involving some kind of haggling between you, your manager and the company overall to set goals that are *stretchy but achievable*. If you're like me, then your gut feel will be to go big: you're sure you can sign up five new clients next quarter, or increase revenue by 20%. And if nothing else, it creates a lofty goal for you to strive for. But really, all that you're potentially doing is creating a rod for your own back — at performance review time, you'll argue that your 15% revenue increase is actually really good (which it is!) but your boss will refer back to your target and therefore say she is sorry, she cannot give you the pay rise / promotion / other goody that you were hoping for. So don't get carried away by your ambition but instead find defensible reasons why a slightly lower target is perfectly appropriate in this context. Then go smash it.[7]

As an aside, target setting is usually quite a drawn out process with a number of last-minute changes as budgets need to

---

7 I'm not saying this is easy, particularly with some bosses who love setting unrealistic targets out of an almost sadistic desire to keep pushing their staff. For more thoughts on this, see the chapter on Managing your boss later.

be made to fit — so you've got to stick to your position until the very end, when everybody else is faltering.

This principle can be applied much more widely than merely at the main goal setting times, by using it more subtly. Here are a few examples:

- Think it'll take you three days to do a certain piece of work? Why don't you tell your boss it will take four, then she'll be pleasantly surprised at your efficiency — unless of course she *knows* it should take three.

- Likely to be ten minutes late for a meeting? Definitely don't say five and disappoint people twice. Instead, say fifteen, apologise profusely, and turn up earlier than expected to start off on the right foot.[8]

- Reckon you need an annual budget of £30k? Try and haggle for £50k then give back some of the money when finance asks for cost cuts later in the year.

- Think a meeting you're organising will take 45 minutes? Please don't say "this should take no more than 45 minutes" and run over a bit. Instead, schedule the meeting for an hour and finish early. Attendees will be delighted about the great meeting with the bonus early ending.

Of course, managing expectations with others doesn't automatically mean lowering the personal goals you set for yourself, or your team if you have one. In fact, having two-track

---

8   An advanced option is saying you might be 5-10 minutes late and turning up on time for a small 'free' bit of goodwill

goaling can be quite an effective way of aiming high while being realistic, as long as it doesn't become too obvious.

Once again, I'm not saying you should forever sandbag every expectation and see what you can get away with. Like most things, it's about finding the right balance and in some circumstances, it's right to push as hard as you possibly can, indeed setting a slightly unrealistic target can spur you on to achieving greater things. On the other hand, formal targets can be very hard to shift once they've been set, so make sure you don't get caught out, particularly if you're compared to someone else who has successfully managed their expectations down.

ACTION

Think of an upcoming piece of work where expectations will need to be agreed — they could be output expectations such as sales, or input expectations such as delivery time or cost. Write down what you think you can achieve if all goes well. Now pick a more realistic goal that you have a high chance of achieving, even if a few things don't go to plan. Finally, write down a few arguments (such as external benchmarks or previous performance) that might convince those overseeing the work that the more reasonable target is the right one.

Keeping focus: The exam question

Not long ago I was put in charge of a work project to evaluate the acquisition of another company. I've done a few of these and they're always really fun, because not only do you get to dissect how the other company works, but you also need to think about post-merger integration and how the combined company might operate.

The first thing I did upon getting the assignment was to put together a project team of great people from across the business — all sworn to secrecy of course. You need a complete picture of your target which means everything from marketing and sales via finance all the way to legal, tax and HR. Only if all — or at least most — of those stars align (and you get a decent price) can you start to think seriously about making an offer.

I was lucky to have a team of experts around me to complete the work — well not entirely lucky as I tried to sweet-talk the best people into coming onto the team, promising them some fun along the way! After a thorough briefing, off they went to analyse their respective areas and report back a few weeks later. Marketing said that the target seemed to have good brand equity but their actual engagement and conversion was poor. Sales thought that they had an interesting boots-on-the-ground approach that we could probably replicate, though it would take time. Finance had a lot of unanswered questions on their accounts but said there might be a way through. Tax had concerns regarding the Chinese subsidiary, legal was missing important clauses in key contracts and HR thought integration was certainly possible but would be pretty messy. Everyone was very motivated, happy to continue chugging away and to report back on their respective questions in a month or two. Meeting adjourned.

The problem was: Collectively we had lost sight of what we were really trying to do — what was the *exam question* we were trying to answer? This wasn't about marketing or tax or legal, although all of those are important contributors. Ultimately, the point of the exercise was to decide whether to buy this company. And it was already becoming clear that, given the large number of issues, the answer almost certainly would be a resounding No. So there wasn't any point in continuing the individual exercises and wasting a huge amount of collective time — exam question answered, job done, even if everyone was quite disappointed because it's a little unusual not to pursue an opportunity[9].

At this point you may ask how this is relevant to your current situation, given that you're unlikely to be leading a company acquisition project. That's because the *exam question* principle applies to almost everything that you do, no matter how big or small. You've been asked to pull together marketing analytics data? Be clear on the actual decision that this will drive (say, how much money we should spend on a certain product line). Are you currently working on a

---

9   Unusual but really important – see *Strategy is deciding what not to do* in Section 4

client profile? Find out what the purpose is — it could be a sales pitch, a product proposal, a CEO meeting. You've been invited to a new meeting next week? Understand its purpose before you show up.

Just as in your school exams, clearly articulating the question you are trying to answer upfront, then using it to keep you on track, is a great way to improve your focus and effectiveness and avoid wasting time on irrelevant work. And as with any real exam question, you should be able to express it in relatively simple terms, so that (say) your parents could understand it even if they don't know much else about your work. This can be particularly tricky if you operate in a pressurised environment with a 'questions just slow us down' vibe, but it's exactly in those environments where being clear on the ask is likely to bring the biggest benefits, so do persevere.

It's also important that your understanding of the exam question is widely shared across the business, because otherwise you might be answering the wrong question! So once you've articulated it for yourself, make sure to share it with your boss or key team members so everyone is fully aligned. For bigger projects, it may be helpful to actually write down this shared understanding either in an email, or if needed, in a 'terms of reference' document outlining objectives and desired outcomes.

Of course, it's not possible to boil down every piece of work to a simple question with a bow on top. Sometimes there are more detailed nuances, but more often these become an excuse for lack of clarity so don't let yourself be fobbed off with jargon-laden waffle. If you don't understand the point of the exercise, you're likely not the only one, so keep pushing. As someone once said to me, "clever people ask complex questions, very clever people ask simple questions".

ACTION

Consider the three projects or pieces of work on which you currently spend most of your time. For each, clearly articulate the exam question: Why are you doing this work? What decision or action will ultimately come of it? Or if you can't, then find out! Finally, share the outcome with key stakeholders to ensure alignment.

Managing time: Trying to avoid 'al desko'

I don't know about you, but I'm not a big fan of sandwiches. Maybe it's my continental upbringing but while they do the trick, there's something inherently depressing about a cold, slightly soggy piece of bread for lunch — particularly if it's consumed as an afterthought while in a meeting or writing an urgent email at your desk. My ancestors would be horrified by the idea of lunch 'al desko'.

But it's often hard to avoid, given the demands on our time — in our personal as well as business lives — have never been greater. There's always one more thing to do, so who's got time to sit down for lunch, even if it's only for 20 minutes?

Now more than ever, good time management is essential, and not just to improve your culinary experience — in my view, it's far more important what you do with the hours that you work than how many hours you clock in the first place. Entire books have been written on how to maximise the value you get from your time, but let's keep it simple initially, and start with a time inventory.

ACTION 1

Think back over your last month at work (either based on memory alone or by looking at an actual calendar). First, please divide 100% of available time into the following rough buckets and jot down a percentage against each one — making sure they all add up to 100%:

- Time spent in group meetings
- Time spent in one-to-one meetings,
- Time spent analysing data or implementing actions
- Time spent reporting on what you're doing, e.g. writing PowerPoint
- Time spent with external parties such as clients or agencies
- Time spent on company engagement channels such as Email, Slack, Messenger etc.
- Time spent doing anything else I haven't thought of

Now, I'd like you to keep to the same headings and estimate the percentage of total value-add derived from each of them, where 'value-add' is loosely defined as achieving your goals for the month or the quarter. Again, the numbers should add up to 100% across all buckets.

MANAGING TIME: TRYING TO AVOID 'AL DESKO'

I know this is a hard exercise, especially the second part. While I'd like you to try and have some grounding in fact, please don't overthink it but rather get to the best you can in five or ten minutes.

At this point, you're probably expecting me to tell you the ideal split between these buckets, but unfortunately that depends on your personal situation — really this exercise is designed to make you reflect rather than give a prescriptive answer. However, from my experience over the last 30 years there are a few general points worth considering in any case:

Group meetings

First in line to save time are normally group meetings, relative to their value-add. Every company I've ever worked for complains that there are too many meetings, yet most people still go along to the meetings regardless, because their bosses told them to or because everyone else is. So I encourage you to take a long hard look at your group meetings and really ask yourself whether there aren't at least a couple that you can do without. Perhaps a colleague can tell you what happened? Or you only attend occasionally? Maybe you can read meeting notes? Or maybe the meeting is no longer necessary at all? Try experimenting here as even a couple of hours saved per week could make a real difference to your productivity (or your ability to hit the gym on a regular basis).

Doing the work vs reporting on the work

At the most basic level, make sure that you get this balance right. In many companies I've worked in, there is so much time spent reporting on what you've done — via presentations, meetings, reports or other means — that precious little time remains for the actual doing.

Some forward-thinking companies like Amazon have forsworn presentations entirely and instead rely on memos (typically 'one-pagers' or 'four-pagers') to crisply summarise thinking. They even allocate reading time at the beginning of meetings, to make sure everyone is on the same page. But most are still addicted to PowerPoint: the more slides, the merrier. And not just the occasional presentation but a never ending cycle of weekly, monthly and quarterly reviews peppered with team meetings, company meetings, financial reporting and so forth.

While clearly some reporting is essential and a well-structured deck can be very powerful (more on that soon), if you currently feel that you're drowning in reporting, then you need to find some way to get your head back above the water. Do you really need to do it all? Can some of it be re-used? What are the expected levels of quality for each piece, i.e., where can you get away with something quick-and-dirty? Once again there are no magic bullets here, but if you don't tackle this head-on, you'll struggle to make time for the more important things.

Company engagement channels

Do you currently use Slack or a similar real-time collaboration tool? Slack and its siblings are both brilliant for productivity but also a disaster for productivity, because those messages keep on coming and the boss often expects an answer within the hour, so you can't just easily switch off.

I haven't seen any formal research on the net impact of Slack but just like Facebook, Insta and so on it really can sap time if you're not careful, because those short minutes soon add up[10]. So as much as you enjoy the sugar rush of engagement (and the distraction from whatever else you're doing), you need to find a way to control it. Ideally, you'd limit yourself to say, three 20-minute slots a day rather than always-on, but if that would make you look bad with your boss then at least figure out which channels do need immediate attention and which can wait until later.

Urgent vs important work

The other way to think about time allocation is dividing work into urgent versus important. Clearly, some activities are both (so will rise to the top) and some are neither (and are unlikely to happen). But there's a big grey zone in the middle and typically, the urgent always trumps the important because, well, it's urgent. Someone's likely to be chasing you, and in any case it feels good to tick something off the to-do list, even if it's relatively small. While the important things might actually be quite hard, so are nice to push out.

---

10 Really, you should receive a weekly notification of time spent on Slack, similar to Screen Time...

ACTION 2

Write down a couple of important activities that you've put off because urgent things always get in the way. What have you been meaning to do for ages that would actually be really useful? And then — you've guessed it — can you find a way of making room for those by putting to one side some of the more urgent, but less important work? Write those items down alongside and put a big cross through them, or a parking sign, if you prefer.

To finish the chapter, here are a few more time management tips for you to try, if you haven't already:

- Block out 'focus time' in your diary that can't be filled with other meetings (although you'll have to work very hard to maintain it).

- Colour code time slots in your diary according to what they are e.g., group meetings, one-to-one meetings, analysis time etc.; this will provide a helpful visualisation.

- Review what you've achieved with your time on a weekly, or even daily basis

- And finally, get comfortable with the fact that some things just won't get done. As long as they're not critical, and you manage expectations, then that's OK

Every ambitious person struggles with time management and unfortunately there's no magic solution, only incremental improvements from making conscious changes and then being disciplined enough to see them through — but these can and do add up. So start small — my objective each week was to have lunch away from my desk three times, and one run after work. What a difference it made! So consider time management an essential skill to be learnt and refined, not an afterthought.

A Brief Interlude on being honest

Here's a tricky question for you: Have you ever lied at work? And if the answer is yes, then why was that? To cover up for a mistake you made? To avoid a particularly annoying piece of work? Just to get rid of the person standing in front of you? We've all been there but the problem with lying is that it's a slippery slope — for one, you might be found out and even if you're not, the next thing you know, you're tangled in your own web of bullshit, from which it can be very hard to escape.

The obvious solution to this is to always tell the truth — no slippery slope, no ethical dilemmas, and you can sleep easy at night basking in your own virtuousness. The problem of course is that this is not how the world works. Just as you're not going to tell your children that really, they are quite rubbish at sports or arts or whatever, you're not going to want to be telling everyone in your workplace what you actually think, all of the time. So, a middle ground is needed and what I'm advocating is to avoid outright lies at all cost (less risk and better karma) but on the other hand, remain suitably vague in what you're saying so that there's enough room for interpretation. The truth, most of the truth and nothing but the truth, if you like.

I realise that this all sounds very theoretical so best to move straight to a practical example. Imagine that you're late for work one morning because you've overslept as you had a late, boozy night. Of course, you could say to your boss: "I'm sorry I'm late, I overslept as I had a night on the tiles." In some situations this may be OK but more likely, you'll just look unprofessional. Alternatively, you could make up an excuse like: "I'm sorry I'm late, but my train was delayed" but that would be a lie and one that could potentially be uncovered by simply checking a train website. So you want to aim for a vaguer middle ground — how about "I'm sorry I'm late, but I had an issue at home this morning"? That's not strictly untrue as oversleeping is indeed an issue you had at home. But it's vague enough that people can project their own interpretation onto your statement (injured cat? row with partner? broken water pipe?) and are unlikely to ask a follow-up question as they probably don't want to hear the answer. And if they do, you can always say you'd rather not talk about it — which is true about the oversleeping too.

Here are a few more examples:

- Late for a meeting because you simply forgot to look at your watch? Try "My previous engagement overran" (your engagement just happened to be writing an email)
- Don't want to join a brainstorm next Thursday? How about "I'm sorry, I have meetings that day" (you do, but only two of them)
- Rather not work with someone on their project? For now, fob them off with "I'm definitely considering it" (though that consideration is making you want to do it even less)

A BRIEF INTERLUDE ON BEING HONEST

Of course, I'm not suggesting that you start obfuscating at every turn, because that'll just be a bit weird and make people suspicious. Quite often, the right move is to own up to your mistake because taking responsibility shows a good level of maturity and will build trust (as long as you learn your lesson so it doesn't become a habit).

But on the occasions where you'd really rather not, try and find that vague middle ground to get out of the situation truthfully but unscathed. You might think that isn't going to work in many situations, but you'll be surprised how malleable language is once you give it a try.

PS: ~~I've never used this technique myself.~~
~~I use this technique all the time.~~
I've even thought about using this technique myself.

Sending emails: Don't be a Boov

If you have young kids, you might have watched the animated film 'Home', in which a cute being called a Boov makes friends with a young girl to save both Planet Earth and the Boov themselves. The film's main protagonist is a slightly hapless Boov called 'Oh' who in one scene sends an email invitation to his house warming party not just to his friend Kyle but instead to *the entire galaxy*, thus giving away the Boovs' location to their arch-enemy the Gorg[11]. Upon realising his mistake, Oh exclaims: "It is not my fault! Whyfor put Send button next to Send All? It's just bad design".

Email mistakes happen to the best of us. Whether it's sending a reply to everyone when you didn't mean to, addressing a message complaining *about* George *to* George instead, misspelling someone's name, pressing send when the message was only half-written (Ctrl-Enter is efficient but dangerous) or simply forgetting that all-important attachment: the possibilities for screw-ups are endless and they therefore happen quite regularly. Most of the time, the effect is harmless — a quick resend (*'with* attachment this time, soz everyone') will do the trick and no one'll actually remember the

---

[11] Spoiler alert: They all become friends at the end. I highly recommend watching the film, even without kids.

issue for more than five minutes. However, occasionally it does become more embarrassing and can lead to ridicule or worse, disciplinary action.

And it's not only mistakes that can have a potentially negative impact on the receiver and by extension, you. That grumpy reply you sent because the email caught you at a bad moment may end up seriously offending someone, needing time and work to rebuild their trust. Shoddy spelling, grammar or sentence construction will make you look unprofessional. Or your email may just be overly long and rambling so that by the end of it, people lose the will to live and don't understand your point.

So I'll let you in on a boring secret: Even after 30 years of use (I first had an email address in 1994 while at university), I still re-read every single email I write before I send it. I'm constantly amazed at how many mistakes the original draft contains: rogue words, half-finished sentences and more often than you'd think, the wrong recipient's name. And that's before talking about the tone and structure of the email, which could do with being improved nine times out of ten.

Of course, some emails only get a relatively brief second glance, if they're short and sent to a trusted colleague. However, the really important ones — say job applications or team broadcasts — go through multiple drafts and are often proofread by others. And as an additional precaution, for extra important ones I won't add the sender's address — or temporarily remove it if it's a reply — until I'm fully happy with the message itself. That way, I can't accidentally send a half finished email. Really boring? Yes. Effective? Also yes.

The other thing that people often forget about emails is that, after all, they are permanent written records and ultimately you can never know 100% where they'll end up. What was meant as an off-the-cuff remark or quickly written in a huff may look very different in the cold light of day (even if the grammar is perfect). I'd thus also encourage you to add a further sense check, which is whether you'd be happy to have your email forwarded to the CEO, purely theoretically speaking. As a test of reasonableness, it ensures that you avoid personal attacks or excessive venting. Better be safe than sorry and keep any vitriol to unwritten conversations — I know we all need to whinge from time to time but best not to record it for posterity.

ACTION

From tomorrow, I want you to always double check your emails before you hit send. This doesn't have to take more than 30 seconds, just quickly verify the To: Field, the Intro and any attachments. Then for the occasional messages with higher importance, add more advanced checking and reviews as you see fit. But that first reflex of holding off before you press send is key — soon it'll be like making sure you have your keys before you leave the house!

Writing presentations: Avoiding 'death by PowerPoint'...

My first experience with presentation software was back in 1997, when I started my career as a strategy consultant for a London-based firm that sadly no longer exists. The whole thing was rather preposterous as I hadn't yet turned 21, looked like 17 and nonetheless was packed off on Day 3 to work full-time at a client site in Holland. I'll never forget the look on my manager's face, seeing me for the first time at Heathrow Airport that Monday morning at 6am. I really didn't have a clue, but somehow it all turned out OK in the end. At least I think it did — we ended up saving the client a lot of money, but at the expense of some local suppliers who were wiped out in favour of larger, global ones. I was certainly not very aware back then!

Anyway, back in the days we didn't use the now-ubiquitous PowerPoint but a little-known programme called 'Solo', which seems to have disappeared entirely, as despite my best efforts I couldn't find a trace of it on the Internet. Solo was very powerful but also very complicated, so that the consulting firm (like most others) employed a dedicated group of presentation creators to whom we would send hand-drawn pages every night, which would be returned as fully-blown slides the next day. The presentation team enjoyed considerable respect within the organisation, not least because they had the power to slow down your output if they so desired. Hence 50+ page Solo decks could be created in the space of a few days so as to successfully bamboozle the client with ever more complex charts.

Today, in most jobs you're unlikely to have a small army of presentation specialists at your disposal — instead, you're generally expected to write your own PowerPoint presentations or perhaps you're lucky enough to have a team working with you to whom you can delegate some of the work. More recently, AI has been making great strides in speeding up some of the process, but nonetheless (unless you work for Amazon, more on that later), you're likely to be spending a reasonable amount of time writing slides. At this point, may I make a humble suggestion: Don't. Avoid it like the plague. In my view, 80% of time spent on slides is wasted, it merely gives you comfort by creating lots of pretty charts. Why? Because despite sucking up lots of time, fundamentally PowerPoint lets you get away with lazy thinking — style over substance, quantity over quality, slides instead of actions.

Ideally, write a memo...

That's all very well, I hear you say, but information needs to be conveyed somehow, so what do you suggest? The answer is relatively simple: instead of PowerPoint, use Word. Instead of preparing a presentation, write a memo!

You might think that memos are a bit old-school, dating from times when the world was black-and-white and the Internet hadn't been invented. They might be, but they're also very powerful because they force you to clearly articulate your thinking in a way that PowerPoint does not. This means that memos often take a long time to craft, but the result will be the better for it. To paraphrase Mark Twain, "I'm sorry I wrote you such a long PowerPoint, I didn't have time to write you a short Memo".

The principles of writing a good memo are very simple in theory, but hard to achieve in practice:

- Always start with a short executive summary outlining key points. Writing this first will help to structure what follows

- Explain the context and where we find ourselves today

- This should lead to the exam question you're trying to answer

- Show the different options you've considered and how they compare

- Say which option you'd recommend and why

- Explain how you'd implement your recommendation; how long it may take and what resources it requires

- If needed, show the key risks and how you are proposing to address them

- And season the whole thing with a few well-chosen charts to illustrate your key points

And if you need additional evidence of the success of memo-based communication, look no further than Amazon's Jeff Bezos, who had this to say in a letter to shareholders: "We don't do PowerPoint (or any other slide-oriented) presentations at Amazon. Instead, we write narratively structured six-page memos. We silently read one at the beginning of each meeting in a kind of study hall. (...) The great memos are written and re-written, shared with colleagues who are asked to improve the work, set aside for a couple of days, and then edited again with a fresh mind. They simply can't be done in a day or two."

After a decade of PowerPoint-driven jobs, I discovered great memo-writing at the hands of my long-time boss at Eurostar, who was a master craftsman. I've used the technique since then to great effect, if nothing else because so few memos are written nowadays that even a moderately good one will stand out in the sea of PowerPoints — and so have more impact more quickly.

...but if you must do PowerPoint, do it well!

Despite my exhortations, you're probably unlikely to avoid PowerPoint entirely, if nothing else because your company requires it. To be fair, it can be useful for more interactive presentations (e.g., to a wider audience) where memos would just be deathly dull. And having said that I'd rather you didn't use PowerPoint, doing it well is a useful life skill that can set you apart from your colleagues. As a CTO I know once said: "In a company where everyone can code, the engineer who can do slides is king".

So reluctantly but importantly, here are my top tips for the successful use of PowerPoint:

1. Before you jump into individual slides, write the executive summary and a 'strawman' outline of your presentation so that you're clear about the

story you wish to tell and what information you need to tell it. You can also use this to get early buy-in from other stakeholders or indeed to ask for their assistance in writing some of the slides! As you do this, your life will be easier if you…

2. Use insightful titles for each slide rather than simple descriptions. So, use '25% revenue drop in Q1 across all markets' rather than 'Q1 revenue overview'. Ideally, just reading the titles of each slide should be enough to understand the story of your presentation. This also helps to…

3. Make sure any charts on your page support the title message. This is harder than it sounds as you may have to change the way the chart is organised! In my example above, you should be able to clearly see a 25% drop somewhere on the chart, rather than having to figure it out for yourself. However, make sure you…

4. Don't get too clever with the charts you're using. Yes, you could get three or four dimensions onto each chart by using bubble sizes or shading, but no one will understand what you're trying to say. Do aim to be a bit clever though — a giant pie chart with four slices isn't going to cut it either. In any case leave some space and…

5. Don't cram the slides full of words but really focus on the essential messages. Here, it depends on whether you're actually presenting the slides or merely circulating them by email. If it's the former, you'll have the best effect by using words quite sparingly so

that your audience gets primed for what you have to say without losing interest in you actually saying it (because they're busy reading the words on the slide.) If it's the latter, you can use a few more words to give context, but even then don't go overboard. In fact...

6. Really think about whether each slide is actually necessary or is only included because you have the information. Entirely unscientific research (by me) shows that after 20 slides at most, people's eyes glaze over and they start thinking about their dinner plans or upcoming holidays. It's much better to spend five minutes on each of ten slides (with a bit of Q&A) than two minutes on each of 25. Once the slides are done, you need to....

7. Prepare for the actual meeting. I get that presenting can be scary but too many people are focused on *getting through their content*, as opposed to *achieving the desired outcome*. Don't see questions or comments as annoying interruptions of your flow — rather, they're great opportunities to engage with your audience. If that means you need to cut some content later on, so be it. But of course it depends on...

8. The Golden Rule: Know your audience! Some people prefer more detail, some less; some prefer graphs and some prefer images. So adapt accordingly. And finally...

9. Follow AI developments closely. Tools such as Canva or ChatGPT can help with structure and layout and will only get better.

Being able to clearly articulate a story into either a memo or a presentation is one of the key skills you'll need to develop to become moderately successful, and I speak from experience to say that true excellence here is a lifelong quest. So the sooner you start to seriously work on each presentation that you write, the better you'll get at it eventually — without ever mastering the art completely.

ACTION

Pick a topic that you need to communicate to others — for example, a progress report you're expected to give or a proposal for investment. Write down the key elements of the story you'd like to tell — the executive summary. Use this draft to create an impactful memo or presentation.

Or if you're already in the process of preparing a presentation, then use the checklist above to improve the quality and impact.

Being proactive: "Einer geht sich immer noch aus"

I'm originally from Austria and grew up in Vienna before moving to the UK aged 17. When I first arrived, I thought the two countries' cultures weren't so different — after all we both like football and beer and used to have empires that were dismantled long ago. I soon discovered that there were more differences than met the eye, and some more subtle than others. One of the most striking of these, which still makes me chuckle today, is the British desire to queue at every suitable opportunity — because it really couldn't be further from the Austrian approach. It's not just that Brits queue in a nice, neat line at places like bus stops (in Austria, there's just a throng) but it's a whole mindset that is practically *looking* for a queue in many situations. Whether it's men's toilets (queuing for cubicles even if urinals are available) or passport control (happily joining the longest queues), it wouldn't cross most Brits' minds to find a shortcut, whereas Austrians are literally programmed to do just that. Perhaps it's the fault of ski lift queues in our youth, but our approach is best summed up when considering a full-looking car park: "*Einer* geht sich immer noch aus", as my friend Phil would put it. "There's always space for *one* more."

By this point you may be hoping not to meet any Austrians any time soon, but I think we can all benefit from *being more Austrian* occasionally, at least in business: more often than you might think, if you don't ask, you don't get. When you're in a tricky business situation where it's hard to get cut-through, don't politely wait until somebody calls your number — don't *join the queue*. Instead, take the opposite approach and think: This looks like a busy place so to get what I want, I'll need to get my elbows out and grab it.

I realise that this comes more naturally to some people than it does to others. You may already suffer from impostor syndrome, so proactively asking for more can be daunting. I suggest building up your courage by scoring a few easier wins first, before moving onto the harder yards of (say) speaking up in a large senior meeting. Here are some things you can try, in rough order of difficulty:

- Proactively schedule a career development meeting with your manager

- Ask for one-to-one feedback on work you've done or presentations you've made, from people that you trust

- Proactively share your views on an issue in offline channels such as email or Slack

- Take available opportunities that no one else seems to want, for example offer to write up notes from a meeting or prepare the agenda for the next one. (For more on this, see 'Step Up' in Section 5)

- Request to join projects in which you're keen to be involved

- Ask to be one of the presenters at the next team meeting or (in time) exec presentation

But the list is endless and the more you stick your neck out, the more likely you are to get the outcome that you deserve. At the end of the day, it comes back to taking ownership of your destiny — sure, some people are looking out for you and some goodness will naturally come your way. But those same people are also busy and opportunities are limited so to some extent, whoever shouts the loudest is more likely to get what they want: it's just human nature.

There's an important caveat here: while proactivity and a certain level of metaphorical queue-jostling are definitely a good thing, you need to do it in the right way as — let's face it — nobody likes an arrogant idiot. I'm not telling you to constantly barge co-workers out of the way to get on that ski lift to success more quickly. On the other hand, if you keep letting everyone sneak past in the hope that eventually there'll be a seat, you might miss out on the best snow. (Enough metaphors for one chapter? Yes, I think you're right.) The key of course is choosing the right approach — steely and determined? Yes. Charming and engaging? Preferably. Annoying and abrasive? No.

Finding this balance is easier said than done — my own mother once described me as 'the most charming egoist she knows', which thinking back on it probably wasn't a compliment! But the good news is that there are relatively easy places to start with and build from, and if you can use a bit of charm then all the better. There's really nothing abrasive about asking your manager for some career development opportunities and volunteering to lead a meeting or a presentation that perhaps isn't anyone's first choice will be perceived as a positive. Even speaking up in meetings can have a very positive impact if you do it judiciously — don't just shout over other people but politely say that you haven't had a chance to speak yet and would like to share your contribution.

So give it a go and see where it takes you. I promise you that more often than not, there *will* be a car parking space available for you even if lots of others have been circling for a while.

ACTION

Identify at least two opportunities to proactively ask for something in the next week that will give you more responsibility or more visibility, even if you were previously afraid to do so. Then write yourself a mini action plan of how to approach it — Who will you ask? How will you do it? What groundwork do you need to do? If needed, run this past a friend or colleague to sense check and get additional comfort that you're on the right track.

Moving on from setbacks: The 5 stages of grief

I recently interviewed for a job that I didn't get. Initially, I didn't particularly think it was for me but as I progressed through the stages I got really excited about both the brand I'd be working for and the opportunities in the role. It began to seem like the perfect fit, the role I'd always been waiting for. I even started to pay my own money to use the brand's services because of how good it was. I thought I had a pretty good connection with the hiring CEO, who in my first interview told me he'd definitely want to see me again — a rare occurrence and obviously a good sign.

Unfortunately, the recruitment process ended up being really drawn out with long periods of radio silence between interviews, which made it mentally challenging as it was hard to gauge where I stood and anyway, it's tricky to stay in high excitement mode for that long. In the end, I was rejected at the 'last two candidates standing' stage on the basis of cultural fit. It really hurt. Yes, the culture was different to that of my previous job but I felt confident that I'd be able to adapt given I had previously experienced a similar work environment. And I was convinced I was the best qualified candidate especially as the brand was expanding from the UK into Europe, something I'd recently done.

For the first day or two, I mostly sat there in silence, trying to process what had just happened and how all the time I'd spent preparing and researching and getting excited had been basically wasted (plus I didn't have a great plan B for a different role). Then for a while I figured there must have been some sort of mistake and then came a whole lot of anger. At the hiring CEO, for not understanding how I *was* a great cultural fit; at the headhunter, for not briefing me better; and at myself for focusing too much on the content of my final presentation and not enough on the delivery. That took about three days to subside, to be replaced by a plan for a bit of clever bargaining — "I'll send the CEO an email to prove my worth", I thought, "and the HR Director too. Then maybe they'll change their mind". While that got me a nice ego-flattering reply, I still didn't get the job. So after a good few days, the only option I had left was to move on, get back in the saddle and contact another round of recruiters and ex-colleagues. Which is exactly what my son had told me to do when I first mentioned the rejection and which of course is the right answer, it's just so bloody hard to do!

If this pattern sounds a little familiar, then that's because most people go through multiple stages when processing an upsetting experience, something that was first documented by Swiss scientist Elisabeth Kubler-Ross and is commonly known today as the '5 stages of grief'. While the research was primarily focused on significant episodes of grief, such as the death of a loved one, the principle applies to upsetting situations of all kinds so is useful to understand in a business context, both to manage your own emotions but also to empathise with those of others.

The 5 stages, in order, are:

Shock: *I don't yet understand what is happening*

Denial: *This is not actually happening, there must be a mistake*

Anger: *How could they / I be so stupid to let this happen!*

Bargaining: *I'm sure there's a way to make it un-happen*

Acceptance: *OK, it's happened. How do I move on from here.*

The most obvious business applications relate to your job itself: not getting a job, promotion or pay rise; losing your job; a major reorganisation or shift in focus. However, we can also go through mini-episodes of dealing with disappointment in other situations such as important meetings that go badly, lost revenue or simply a human error leading to a business issue.

In my experience, people do experience all 5 stages in the above order, particularly for major setbacks but even for more minor ones: Think about how you'd react to, say, having made a big mistake in an important presentation. The key therefore is to try and move through the process as quickly as possible, while of course still respecting the emotions at play. At the end of the day, the disappointment is unlikely to be un-done so the most effective way to move forward is to accept that it's happened and focus on the future, rather than dwelling on the past. Of course this is easier said than done:

while people normally move through Shock and Denial relatively quickly, they can get stuck in Anger for a very long time, so this is the key stage to address.

Finally, for work situations, I would add a sixth stage — that of post-grief learning. Once you've overcome your disappointment, make sure you use the experience as an opportunity to improve for next time, rather than blaming somebody else or indeed 'the system'. Board presentation go badly? Be better prepared next time, when it really matters. Promotion didn't work out? Spend more time understanding the decision making process (see Section 5 for more on this). Didn't get the job you wanted? Understand why the company felt that way and address this next time.

I very much hope that you won't go through any major trauma at work and want to stress that true grief can take a very long time to overcome whereas work setbacks can normally be dealt with in a few days or weeks at most. However, realising when you or a colleague is going through the stages described above, and trying to avoid getting stuck for too long in any one stage, can be a useful way to improve both productivity and happiness.

ACTION

Choose a disappointment or setback at work that has made you angry. It may also be that really you're more angry at yourself for not doing a good enough job than you are at someone else for treating you badly.

Once you've identified the issue, can you try and find a way to get over it? It's hard to advise on exactly how as dealing with emotions is very personal, but generally talking about your anger with someone else and then channelling it into a constructive plan for the future (so learning from what happened rather than dwelling on it) is a useful way out of a potentially tricky situation.

Finding balance: The Stockdale Paradox

My son started playing football from a young age and while the organising club supplies a qualified referee, one of each side's parents is normally asked to 'run the line', i.e. assist in calling offside and throw-in decisions. One day I offered to step in and actually quite enjoyed it so it became a regular occurrence, so much so that last year I decided to take the step to become a qualified referee myself. Now, 'qualified' is a bit of an overstatement here as this involved attending an eight-hour course with a load of keen 14-year-olds before being let loose on unsuspecting under-12s.

I've watched football on TV for as long as I can remember and then assisted with refereeing for a good five years. Plus, given the 30+ year age gap between me and the kids, I started off with a good dose of inherent authority coupled with a strong and booming voice. So I felt very confident that I'd do well. Then came the night before my first match and I could barely sleep. Did I actually know all the rules? What if I made a big mistake and my authority evaporated? Would I be swayed by players or coaches complaining?

This is but a tiny illustration of what Jim Collins calls *The Stockdale Paradox* in his book Good To Great[12]: The ability to

---

12 See Further Reading for more details

be both supremely confident in your abilities yet very aware of your limitations, at the exact same time. Or as Collins puts it, "you must maintain unwavering faith that you will prevail in the end, regardless of the difficulties, and at the same time have the discipline to confront the most brutal facts of your current reality."

Finding this *balance* between two potentially competing extremes is key. Swing too far one way and you just become arrogant and lazy and will soon enough trip up, or if against the odds you're successful then no one will like you for it. Swing too far the other and you'll drown in worries that everything will fall apart any minute, or if it doesn't you won't be able to enjoy it.

As you might expect, human nature is such that people tend to fixate far more on the latter (all the things that could go wrong) than the former (how great they are), with even the more successful people I know quickly assuming the worst despite their excellent track record of delivery and performance. This is particularly the case for those among you who are *A-Type personalities*, described by Wikipedia as 'high-achieving workaholics who tend to set high expectations for themselves but experience more job-related stress and less job satisfaction'.

Let's take a few work examples:

- Imagine you've been asked to give a presentation on a familiar topic. Of course you should worry about making mistakes, stumbling over words or missing an important point, and minimise those through good preparation. But you also need to take strength from the fact that you're the expert and people want to hear what you have to say!

- Let's say a senior executive has asked you for your opinion on an important project. Do make sure that you gather all the facts and prepare your answer thoroughly, but take confidence from having been asked because it shows that your judgment is respected.

- More generally, you may have impostor syndrome and think that you're underqualified for your current job, or the next one up. Of course, address any obvious shortcomings but also acknowledge that your hiring was the result of a thorough process (not an accident), you have the required experience and your colleagues aren't perfect either.

Overall, it's really important to remind yourself occasionally (particularly if you're A-Type) that you *are* good at what you do and you *will* reach your desired level of success! While at the same time acknowledging that it won't be easy, that it'll take some time to get there and that both great highs and deep lows are part of the journey — or as Rudyard Kipling puts it: "If you can meet with triumph and disaster; and treat those two impostors just the same".

ACTION

First, get yourself two pieces of paper. On one of them, write in big letters: 'I am brilliant. I will prevail.' And on the other, in slightly smaller letters, write: 'There are a lot of problems to fix. Let's get on with it.' Then at least once a week, I'd like you to just look at these two statements and make sure that your balance between the two is right because both statements are true at all times.

Second, in the space below write 'Why I'm brilliant and will prevail' and then list at least five reasons why this is true, so you can remind yourself if necessary. I'm not going to ask you to list your problems as I'm willing to bet that you already know those so don't need reminding as much.

PART 3

HOW TO WORK WITH OTHER PEOPLE

When I worked at Eurostar, we sometimes joked that it'd be an easy job if it wasn't for all those pesky customers and their high expectations. Needless to say, they were the ones that ultimately paid our wages! And anyway I quite enjoyed dealing with confused American tourists or excited kids going to Disneyland, though less so grumpy executives on an expense budget.

You might sometimes feel the same about your colleagues — this would be a great place to work if it wasn't for all those people getting in the way...although some of them are great fun, really.

Of course, those colleagues aren't going anywhere anytime soon, but the good news is that you can learn how to influence them to your advantage — and not just the annoying ones either, but indeed all your internal and external stakeholders. Because just as being good at your job in isolation is a prerequisite for *moderate success*, so is knowing how to work with other people. It's probably more important because you'll need those people to get many things done and some of them will be responsible for deciding your pay rises and promotions.

The thing is, working with other people isn't as easy as you might think. Surely, if your work is good and you're nice enough, then others will just cooperate and be suitably dazzled by your brilliance? Unfortunately not, because, well, life is complicated. People are complicated. It's not a straight line from input to output but a squiggly one defined by who people are, what they want, how they feel, and what they had for breakfast, among many other inputs.

Hence, to work well with other people you need to understand them not superficially, but deeply, so that's where we'll start this section. We'll then move on to using that newly gained understanding to face various counterparts, including your boss, third parties and those people in the company that you'd really rather avoid, via sections on humility, making people feel special and swearing. We'll finish with a piece on active listening, a surprisingly rare skill that can really help you unlock other people.

Hopefully, as you enter the realm of *psychology for beginners*, you'll get excited by the fascinating world of complexity out there and agree that figuring people out will make your job a lot more fun as well as successful.

Understanding people (1): What they do

If you think about it, the idea of a company is a little odd. You throw together tens, hundreds, sometimes thousands of people who barely know each other and expect them to collectively solve problems and produce output that somehow means that at the end of the year, you're better off than where you started and there is profit left over to invest.

Not only do those people often come and go quite frequently (in some companies, turnover can be over 50%), but for the modern company to function it must have many different departments with vastly different points of view to ensure all bases are covered. Product, tech and operations are needed to build and maintain things; marketing, sales and customer service to find and keep people to buy those very things; finance and procurement to make sure the numbers add up; legal, compliance and risk to save the company from shooting itself in the foot and of course HR to keep the whole thing humming.

While there are shared company values, annual targets and hopefully an inspiring mission to bind companies together and grease the wheels, the standard setup can often lead to intense frustration as you run into colleagues who just *don't seem to get it*. "Why can't you just approve my project?!", you shout at legal or finance (hopefully, only in your head) unless you're in legal or finance, in which case you really wish colleagues weren't quite so cavalier with the company's resources. You regularly entertain your friends down the pub with stories about the inflexible morons in *[insert department]* who just want an easy life, and best not to get you started on *[insert irritating person]* in *[worst department ever]*.

It may be true that some people simply enjoy making your life difficult or really just don't understand what's going on (more on working with idiots later). However, in most cases how people behave can be quite rationally explained by their *motivations and incentives* — what drives them, either from a personal perspective or driven by the work context in which they operate. The legal person is being 'difficult' because their job is to make sure that the salesperson doesn't do anything so stupid as to get the company or the CEO sued. The operations person is being inflexible because providing a different product for every single customer would cost a fortune and take forever, so there has to be some standardisation. And finance needs to make sure that all those promises of extra revenue tomorrow, in return for cash outflows today, actually add up.

In fact, some healthy tension between the different departments of a company is perfectly normal and indeed desirable, because it reins in any excesses and ensures that sensible trade-offs are found. As techies like to say: It's a feature, not a bug, of being in a company! Therefore, the first step in working well with other people is to understand their motivations, so you know why they're acting as they are. Only then can you effectively try to work with, and potentially influence, them to help achieve your goals. As hard as it may sometimes seem, try to put yourself in the other person's shoes and understand where they're coming from — what drives them to act in this way? As I said, the answer is likely to be a combination of their work selves (i.e., what department they work in and what their objectives are) and their personal selves (i.e., what their intrinsic values and motivations are). Because it's easier and more predictable, let's start with their role in the business: Here's a handy (if tongue-in-cheek) guide to understanding — and winning over — the key departments in a typical company.

PRODUCT

- **What motivates them:** Designing and building a beautiful product or service that makes them proud, is based on customer insight and has not been rushed. Despite their protestations to the contrary, whether the output is actually useful to customers is less crucial, and low usage will often be blamed on the 'user error' of customers not understanding things properly.
- **How to win them over:** Don't say that customers are right to complain because as a customer yourself you couldn't figure it out either. Instead, throw the question back at them in terms of how usage and satisfaction could be improved. Also, at least pretend to be interested in the nitty-gritty of the production process.

TECHNOLOGY

- **What motivates them:** Doing cool things with technology that their friends will admire, be

it writing software, designing architecture or managing hardware. Being in complete control of all technology decisions around the organisation, particularly as most other employees haven't a clue so they have nearly unfettered power. Letting their rebellious side shine through, for example by flouting the company dress code.
- **How to win them over:** Start by treating them as interesting human beings rather than slightly awkward geeks. Try and understand the basics of how your company's tech actually works before you make a request. Don't wait until something breaks before you speak to them.

SALES

- **What motivates them:** One thing and one thing only, which is hitting their sales targets — partly because their take-home pay depends on it but also because their reputation as a salesperson depends on it. Salespeople will pretend otherwise, but they'd happily sell their grandmother for the right price so they don't usually ask too many questions (such as: can the company actually deliver what is being promised; is it definitely legal) when a sale is imminent.
- **How to win them over:** Help them hit their target, or if that doesn't work (for example, because they keep 'selling the wrong thing') then change their incentive structure so it's aligned with your objectives. Also, showing some empathy for how tough it is to hit the targets.

MARKETING

- **What motivates them:** Creatively, designing beautifully crafted advertisements, preferably with the help of an uber-hip creative agency located in Buenos Aires suggesting 'world-first' deployments, such as wrapping the entirety of Bank tube station in cellophane. Analytically, improving their key metrics such as the ranking on Google Search or the number of Facebook likes. Also, they'd love to win one of the many industry awards on offer.
- **How to win them over:** Definitely don't offer your personal opinion on their work, such as "I didn't like the font" or "are you sure this is the right strapline". Instead, get them excited by asking what marketing they'd really like to do if they had an even larger amount of money than they already do.

CUSTOMER SERVICE

- **What motivates them:** They can be quite a cynical bunch, and often for good reason seeing as they have to sort out all the problems created by other departments, often using systems that don't work very well. They do enjoy actually being allowed to solve customer issues, even if this potentially costs a fortune, as well as being included in discussions about customer facing changes early in the process.
- **How to win them over:** Empathise with the fact that they're the unsung heroes on the front line of customer anger, while often being the last to find out about

customer facing changes. Actually listen to what they have to say, as you'll learn a lot about customers.

FINANCE

- **What motivates them:** Avoiding any surprises with regard to the P&L, such as too much cost or too little revenue, often to the point of paranoia. Avoiding any surprises when it comes to managing both the CEO's and investors' expectations. Keeping departments honest when it comes to spending, based on the (not entirely untrue) assumption that a lot of it is wasteful and if it wasn't them, the company would already be out of business as all the cash would have been frittered away on frivolous projects with little tangible benefit.
- **How to win them over:** Keep finance in the loop about your plans from an early stage to — you guessed it — avoid surprises at all cost. Produce decent business cases with numbers that actually make sense. Occasionally, give unspent money back as well as asking for more, but don't do it too often or you'll be accused of sandbagging.

LEGAL

- **What motivates them:** Eliminating any risk to the organisation by covering all eventualities in a contract, even if some of them only have a minute chance of ever happening. In doing so, outsmarting their counterparts in other organisations. Unfortunately, as those counterparts have exactly the same

motivations, this can gum up the process and make even the simplest agreements take forever.
- **How to win them over:** Marvel at their cleverness in having spotted so many possible booby traps, but then quietly ask them to classify them into low / medium / high likelihood of actual explosion. You'll most likely find the 'high' category relatively empty, allowing you to move on more quickly. Remember that at the end of the day the Legal team are normally advisers, not approvers, though you ignore their recommendations at your peril.

HR

- **What motivates them:** At the more basic level, stopping employees from doing stupid stuff by getting them to follow HR procedures on things like hiring, firing and promotion. This isn't unreasonable because people do a lot of stupid stuff if you let them, which can quickly become very expensive or worse, a PR disaster. At the more advanced level, getting employees excited by defining well-intentioned but oft-ignored HR principles such as employer brands, company values and leadership principles.
- **How to win them over:** Even if you want to fire Geraldine NOW because she's utterly useless, try to follow HR procedures or at minimum alert the HR team if you're planning on ignoring them. They hate few things more than having to clean up other people's messes and in any case you can outsource a lot of the boring paperwork to them so why

wouldn't you. As a bonus, mention how inspired you feel by the recent change in company values.

In most cases, even if you don't agree with how a colleague approaches a question, there is a legitimate motivation lurking somewhere and just restating what you need (but more forcefully), rather than understanding someone's objections, will get you nowhere or worse, could cause lasting damage. Indeed, the more fundamentally opposed you are in your motivations and beliefs to the other person, the more important it is to actually understand where they're coming from!

Hopefully, in time you'll find that a more conciliatory approach — or better, becoming friends with people in other departments — is not only useful in advancing your interests, but also gives you a more rounded perspective on what makes a good company tick, allowing you to come up with more balanced proposals that have a higher chance of being successfully implemented. Don't worry though, there'll still be plenty to moan about down the pub.

ACTION

Write down a department in your business with which you seem to be having regular disagreements, leading to frustration on both sides. Then write down a recent example and try to put yourself in the other department's shoes to understand their motivations — why did they react the way they did? Finally, write down options for a more conciliatory approach aiming for a win-win outcome fulfilling both your and their needs. Then tomorrow, put it into practice.

Working with third parties

Are you a Netflix subscriber? A few years ago, I reckon your answer would have been instantaneous, "why wouldn't you be"? For something like £8 a month you'd get a huge amount of great content plus you can share the account with your friends, so it doesn't really cost you £8 anyway.

Nowadays I'm not so sure. Subscription prices have nearly doubled, content is arguably getting blander, product placement is out of control, and it costs extra if you want no ads or more than two screens at a time. Why would Netflix do all this and jeopardise their success? The answer once again leads us back to incentives and motivations. Netflix is a public company that has only one product and after years of making losses is under big pressure to improve profitability. The executives at Netflix need to make that happen and will have set their various underlings a number of aggressive targets, such as: double revenue from product placement; increase average spend per user by 25%; reduce average cost per show by 25%[13]. And as a result, you're getting a deal that's a lot worse than it used to be and Netflix makes a lot more money — assuming they don't lose too many subscribers in the process! You might not like it, but it's certainly based on rational incentives.

---

13 These are totally made up, but probably not that far from the truth

WORKING WITH THIRD PARTIES

As an aside (just because I find it interesting), Apple, Disney and Amazon have different motivations and hence different strategies, which can be roughly summarised as:

- **APPLE:** Produce high-quality original content to bolster the brand and sell Apple One bundles (but as Apple is still swimming in cash, don't expect aggressive tactics anytime soon)
- **DISNEY:** Prove that subscriptions can make at least as much money as selling and renting content did previously (so do expect more aggressive tactics, although subscriber numbers are still more important at this stage)
- **AMAZON:** Have content just about good enough to keep people locked into their Amazon Prime subscriptions and hence buying most of their stuff from Amazon (so don't expect price increases but don't expect much better content either)

While the chance of you dealing directly with any of Amazon, Apple, Disney or Netflix as part of your job is low (though who knows), the principle of understanding incentives remains the same for any third party that you do encounter. These can include those paid by your organisation (suppliers, contractors, consultants and agencies), those who pay you (your customers!) and those where no direct payment changes hands such as partners, government or regulatory agencies and trade bodies.

Given that there are no shared company values or annual targets that bring you together with external partners, getting under their skin is arguably even more important than when you work with someone internally. So for each third party, ask yourself the following question: *What's in it for them* — what are *their* goals? And how can you establish a win-win relationship? That way, you'll have a much better chance of finding common ground and possible trade-offs. To illustrate, here are a few specific points to bear in mind:

Agencies & consultancies need to make money, too

Let's say you've retained a marketing agency, but you don't like the work they've done for you. Surely, they should just start over and do the work again? Unfortunately, it's not quite as easy as that. Typically, agencies and consultancies will have built their cost proposal around a certain number of hours invested — after all, people are their main cost item and there needs to be enough profit left over at the end of the day to pay for those swanky offices and senior staff bonuses. Therefore, if your hours have been 'used up', the partner on the project will go into the red on their profitability and that is Not A Good Thing for them. It's unlikely you'll be left entirely in the cold, given that the agency wants to protect their reputation, but just asking for ever more revisions is unlikely to get you very far and you should aim to find some reasonably face-saving way out for both parties. Maybe you could pay a little extra but get a much better piece of work?

A smaller profit margin could get you worse quality

In the same vein, if you've managed to negotiate your supplier cost or agency fees down to the bare minimum, there won't be much room left for any free extras. If all you're doing is buying standardised widgets, then that's fine (although even then it's rarely a good idea to push suppliers so hard that they end up losing money), but if you're looking for something a little more customised then be careful how far you push third parties. It might be better to pay slightly more but get a much better product (and a nicer relationship to boot, as you won't be resented every time you speak to them).

Big fish in small pond or small fish in big pond?
Unless you've got a huge budget, you might face the choice of picking a better-known company for whom you're a small client, or a newer one for whom you're one of the biggest. Weigh up the pros and cons — you'll have more leverage over smaller suppliers, but the level of quality could be lower.

But if you pay money, then don't forget that you're the client!
Having said all this, when dealing with suppliers always remember that you're the client and you're the one paying for goods or services to be delivered. Don't let agencies get away with substandard work, generic excuses or allocating only the most junior members of their team. If any of that is happening, even if the supplier in question is called Google or McKinsey or Apple or 'hottest agency in town', then call them out on it directly or ask your senior person to. Some suppliers may not like (or be used to) hearing negative feedback but often, whoever shouts the loudest is likely to get better service, especially for larger companies with hundreds of clients. Don't exploit the power dynamic by being unnecessarily mean but do use the leverage that you have to its full extent so you're not taken for a ride.

Establish industry networks

Looking beyond just suppliers to the wider industry that you work in, have a look around to see with whom it might be useful to establish good relationships — perhaps a functional expert, an industry body or even a competitor. Find the people that are more altruistic, helpful, or capable than others, then befriend and help them. Forming a strong bond with a network of capable people across an industry can help everyone within that group succeed faster.

ACTION

Write down the name of an external organisation or individual with whom your relationship could be improved. Spend a few minutes jotting down their motivations — what does success look like for them in this relationship? Then identify any leverage that you have to create a win-win situation where both of you can be happy. Finally, write a plan of action of how you'll implement your idea.

Understanding people (2): Who they are

Departments, job titles and company names are useful shortcuts to understanding people because they do, to some extent, sort themselves into areas that are more suitable to their way of working — you're just less likely to encounter an introverted salesperson or a gregarious lawyer. However, it's clearly nonsense to say that everyone in finance or marketing thinks exactly the same or that once you've understood one engineer, you've understood them all. And that's because actions aren't only driven by what people do, but also who they are as a person and the experiences that have shaped them.

These are of course harder to figure out given that you can't look them up on the company intranet, but there are still pointers you can use to build a more rounded picture of each individual. While these will require a bit of time, you can dial the investment up or down according to the importance of each relationship.

BEHAVIOURAL PROFILES

In the first section about understanding yourself, we spoke about various personality inventories such as the MBTI and the 'colour wheel'. While these are useful to understand your own drivers, they can equally be used to understand how others think and operate, thus informing how you approach them. While the test results may not be openly available (although sometimes they are), it shouldn't take you too long to hazard an informed guess. You can always ask a friend for confirmation if you're unsure, which incidentally is quite a fun parlour-game to while away some time in the office!

Let's take the colour wheel and say you're a Fiery Red profile, someone who's rational and determined and just wants to get on with doing things. (That would be me!) And let's say you have to work with a colleague who's Sunshine Yellow and thus fizzes with new ideas that they love to discuss with others. Organisations need both of these traits to thrive, but as a Red your gut reaction will be to tell the Yellow that their ideas aren't properly thought through so won't work, and anyway there are way too many of them so can we please just get back to work. Conversely the Yellow might retort that your rational plans are all well and good, but more of the same just isn't going to cut it, and we're losing ground to the competition by standing still.

Talking past each other won't get you very far, so to be more effective you'll have to adapt your ways of working. Here's a handy shortcut guide of how to deal with each preference[14]:

- **Cool Blue** (data-driven introverts): Lead with detail, accuracy and quality. Give time to reflect.
- **Earth Green** (value-driven introverts): Lead with people and values. Give time to reflect.

---

14 A lot more information on this is available online, if you look for 'Insights Discovery®'.

- **Fiery Red** (data-driven extroverts): Be direct, action- and results-focused. Show quick wins.
- **Sunshine Yellow** (value-driven extroverts): Give space for ideas, collaboration and socialising.

Or if pigeon-holing people into a single colour is too much for you, you can use the individual MBTI axes as a handy alternative: as a reminder these are (1) introverted vs extroverted; (2) big picture vs detail; (3) thinking vs feeling and (4) planned vs spontaneous. Friction will occur if you are on opposite ends of any of those axes; if so, try and adapt your behaviour accordingly. Sounds relatively straightforward in theory, actually doing it in practice might require a significant amount of self-control!

SENIORITY

Particularly in larger companies, it's my experience that more senior people (Directors and above, but particularly very senior people such as CEOs and CFOs) tend to exhibit certain common traits that, if you need to deal with them more regularly, are worth noting. These can include:

- A belief that they are always right and that their ideas are genius
- A (connected) refusal to accept that they were wrong, even if it's clearly the case
- An uncanny ability to 'drink their own Kool-Aid' (i.e., believe in their own stories) to the point of obsession
- A very short attention span

- And a strong desire to project a perfect image externally, always

Before accepting these as gospel, you should of course verify their applicability to your particular situation by observing people's actual behaviours — and it should be easy to compare notes with others, who will likely have made their own observations.

I'm afraid there is some bad news here: If some of the above are indeed true, and if you find some of them difficult to deal with, then it'll have to be you who needs to adapt and not the other way around. This doesn't need to mean selling out your values or being overly deferential (even most senior people don't like overt sucking up, although some do). It does however mean that, as the French would say, you need to *caresser dans le sens du poil*. (Literally, *stroke in the direction of the hair*, a metaphor made easier if you think of the CEO as a cat.)

The key to influencing senior people, then, is not necessarily what you say but how you say it. Don't say the CEO's idea won't work, but build on it to make it better (or completely different by the end). Don't say "I told you so" when something doesn't go to plan — they'll likely know it anyway — but subtly use your newfound respect to influence the next decision. Don't be offended, but be proud, if the senior person repackages one of your ideas as their own. Do speak up but know your place (such as a friend of mine who was offered a ride on the private jet of his uber-rich employer and when he sat down in a free seat was told "You'll be more comfortable…at the back of the plane.") And never, ever, make them look bad, particularly in front of larger audiences.

There are special considerations to working with your immediate boss that we'll come to in a chapter shortly.

THE INDIVIDUAL BEHIND THE LABELS

Of course, to establish true relationships based on mutual trust — say with your closest colleagues or a person whom you particularly need to influence — you'll need to invest the necessary time to understand their personal drivers in even more detail, at an individual level. What has really shaped them as a person? What are their political views? What's most important to them about coming to work in the morning? What's their family situation like?

For this you'll have to go beyond labels such as job title, behavioural profile or seniority, and you can do this either by simply observing someone's ways of operating, their likes and dislikes, what seems to get them excited, what they say and do. Alternatively, and this is really your only option to get to the deepest drivers, you'll need to actually spend some time with the person in question to get to know them better. Suggest going out for lunch or coffee or just spend a few minutes at the end of a meeting to inquire into their family or interests. Over time, you'll build a much more rounded picture of the person in question, which will help you understand their motivations but also build a much better rapport. And you never know, you might make a friend for life.

IN CONCLUSION

Especially if you're more of a thinking introvert than a people-driven extrovert, this chapter might feel a little overwhelming. So many drivers. So many possible hooks. So much work to do to understand them. That's at least how I used to think of it when I first started work. Why can't everyone just operate the way I do? That'd just be a lot easier!

Unfortunately, that's not how the world works and in fact I'd like to encourage you to think about it the other way around. So many exciting personalities to discover. So many layers to each one. So many mini fist bumps when you make a true connection. If you consider it a treasure hunt rather than a chore, then understanding and subsequently influencing people who are very different can be tremendously interesting, plus you'll learn something about yourself in the process. It won't be easy, but it's worth the effort.

ACTION

Write down the names and job titles of two colleagues with whom you'd like a better relationship. Have a guess at their behavioural profiles and write down anything else you know about what drives them. Then, depending on how this compares to your own preferences, think of how you might approach your next conversation with them to achieve a better outcome.

Showing humility: Three men go camping

My son and I have just returned from camping in Dorset with two of his friends and their dads. At the risk of sounding old, I have quite a romantic view of camping as an opportunity to spend a few nights under the stars with only a rucksack on your back, toasting marshmallows over a campfire, eating tinned sausages and, if you were lucky, a small bottle of 'Schnaps' to finish off. In the morning, you'd let a steaming cup of tea slowly bring you back to life while you listen to birdsong and plan the day ahead.

If you've been to a campsite recently, you'll know that when people invite you to go camping, that's rarely what they mean. In place of a lush field with a simple tap and loo, I found a burger van and a farm shop, and all around us bright orange electrical sockets beckoned visitors to attach their myriad gadgets. Instead of an escape to a simpler, less complicated life, camping has become the new way of impressing the neighbours with the latest technology. Putting up a tent by hand? Not if you have inflatable poles and an electric pump. Pasta and warm beer for dinner? Your portable fire pit, hotplate and mini fridge will see to that. Singing songs by the fire? The latest film projected onto a makeshift screen is far more enticing.

It was made all the worse by the absence of women in our group. Not only was there an excess of gadgets, there was also the unbridled desire of each alpha male to demonstrate their unsurpassed ability to use them. From the exact angle in which to pitch a tent into the wind to the perfect way to barbecue a chicken wing, everyone knew exactly what to do and was certainly not going to take any advice from anyone else. Of course, infallibility wasn't limited to gadgets but extended to map reading and cloud-based rain forecasting too. Combined with a tendency to tell tall tales from the past ("once I had to chase away a bear..."), humility was in desperately short supply.

Unfortunately, as it is with camping, it is often in office environments too. Everyone is an expert on everything, even if they really haven't got a clue — particularly men. More often than not, people are afraid to admit that they don't know how to do something, as they're worried about losing face, and humility goes out the window. Of course, I'm not saying that you shouldn't believe in your abilities or undersell yourself: If you really are a whiz at PowerPoint or amazing at creating financial models, then make sure the message is heard loud and clear and soon enough, your co-workers will seek out your expertise in these areas.

At the same time, if you don't really know the answer to a question or the best way of doing things, then be upfront about it and say so. It'll avoid awkward conversations later when the truth eventually comes out, plus you'll actually learn something along the way. Trust me, after they've overcome their initial shock, your colleagues will find it surprisingly refreshing when you admit that no, you're not an expert on French legal matters and that really we should ask someone who is.

I know this may sometimes feel uncomfortable, particularly if you think that what you're asking is a *stupid question*. To give you confidence in asking it anyway, here is my totally unscientific estimate of what happens when you ask what you believe is a stupid question:

- 50% of the time, the question is relatively basic, but people will be very happy to patiently explain the answer. Hence, you'll gain a bit of kudos for your humility and you'll make others feel good for looking knowledgeable.

- 45% of the time, the question is actually rather insightful and one that others have been meaning to ask for ages but were too scared to. Hence, you'll gain major kudos for your humility and bravery.

- Only 5% of the time is the question truly a little stupid and everyone looks at you mildly baffled. You might lose a bit of kudos but people will have forgotten by the next day.

When you add to this the benefit of getting the answer to your question (rather than staying confused) then I think on balance it's definitely worth sticking your neck out and asking. Even if it does take a little bravery, you'll be better off overall.

ACTION

Write down a stupid question that you've been meaning to ask for a while, then figure out where you could best ask it. Now all you need to do is to pluck up the courage and actually do it!

A Brief Interlude on swearing

I have a confession to make: I like swearing. Not spittle-from-the-mouth shouting *at* people, but the occasional use of a swearword to describe and amplify a point. Of course, whether swearing at work is acceptable depends on the culture and the context, so you have to be very careful (and possibly a bit senior in the organisation) to get away with it[15]. However, it's also a natural thing that most people do outside of work, so barring it from the workplace entirely has always felt odd to me.

To me, swearing is quite cathartic and I learnt recently that people who swear while exercising will expend 12% more effort than those who don't, so that's one benefit at least. It's also often the most concise way to express an emotion, particularly using the word 'fuck'. Looking at it in print like this, it's a bit shocking, isn't it? Like it really should have some **s instead of spelling it out. But few words are quite as versatile as 'fuck', which can show surprise, dismay, pleasure and awe amongst other things.

Likewise 'shit', which strangely enough often has positive connotations — I still remember my summer job at Morgan Stanley in New York where "I have some shit to show you"

---

15 Unless you work in an office where everyone swears all of the time, in which case you might want to consider alternative career options...

was a genuine offer of help. Or consider one of Deliveroo's early company values: 'Give a shit'. They've removed it now but I'm not joking, it was there, and while it might be a little shocking, doesn't it feel a lot more impactful than the bland alternatives of 'Obsess about operational excellence' and 'Be curious'? (Incidentally, the tech company Atlassian has 'Don't fuck the customer' as one of their values — no really, they do — which even I think might be going too far).

Clearly, I'm not suggesting that every other word you utter should henceforth be a swearword. However, done judiciously, swearing will have quite a big impact. For example, as a collective escape valve when there's been some external event: It'll establish a deeper bond with your colleagues, because they'll feel the same but are too timid to express their feelings out loud. Or to show that you're really impressed by someone's work: They'll certainly remember that compliment. Or to add extra emphasis when something's just not good enough (but be *very* careful with that one so it doesn't feel like you're insulting a person directly).

If you don't swear often then people will definitely remember when you do, so consider it another weapon in your arsenal for when you really need to have an impact. Just don't fucking overdo it.

Understanding people (3): Where they're from

A little while ago, I was leading the project to launch a new train service between London and Amsterdam. For technical and political reasons, it's a more complex undertaking than you might imagine and involved people from Holland, Belgium, France, Germany and the UK. My initial focus, once the participants had been identified, was to get them to actually work together, despite the fact that many of them had never met.

If you've only worked in the UK, you'll probably think that this sounds a little tricky but not impossible — just get them all round the table first and down the pub second, and they'll be best friends in no time. Unfortunately, that's not how it works on the continent. Despite 75 years of *détente*, you'll find deep-rooted scepticism in a German that any good will come from working with the French and vice-versa; the Belgians are worried about being overlooked; the Dutch are friendly but a bit in-your-face; and in any case nobody really understands what the Brits are on about. To boot, there's often lots of organisational baggage, so even if people want to be helpful they are hamstrung by the context in which they operate.

At this point you have some options. You could pretend all these differences don't exist and proceed as you would at home — just invite everyone to a meeting, be nice and open, buy them a drink and hope for the best. Or, you could go the other way: throw your hands in the air and have a good whinge about how annoying each country is and if only the French weren't so bloody French life would be a lot simpler. I would recommend a third option, which is to embrace the cultural differences and use them to your advantage!

This is because two things turn out to be true. The first is that cultural stereotypes remain surprising valid, seeing as they are driven by national norms. ("Heresy!", I hear you scream, "deep down we're all the same". Perhaps, but up above cultural differences are alive and kicking.) The second is that those stereotypes aren't all that difficult to understand and use to your advantage. To help with this, here is a quick introductory guide to the major European nationalities from a business perspective. Of course, it's a crass oversimplification: for example, you'll find identikit strategy consulting types in all countries. But it's better to be prepared for the 'worst' and then be pleasantly surprised at how similar people are to you, than to go in all bull-in-a-china-shop and be disappointed at the lack of results. So here we go.

THE FRENCH

- As a general rule, it takes a lot more work to establish a trusting relationship with the French than with most other nationalities. Possibly this is caused by the French having a healthy suspicion of foreigners but certainly French working environments feel more cliquey and thus harder to penetrate. So, you'll really need to put the effort in to understand your counterparts and what drives them. It took me almost

three months to get invited out for a drink when I worked in Paris, by contrast in London it took about three hours! However, when you do succeed you're likely to have a strong and trusting relationship for life.
- By and large, businesses still operate in quite a hierarchical and bureaucratic manner, so be sure to do things in the proper way. If you'd like to have a meeting with a mid-level person, don't ask them directly but instead ask your boss to ask their boss whether it's OK to go ahead (you might need to go two or more bosses up in some cases). Otherwise, either the meeting won't happen or it will but you might not receive the information you expected.
- The need for formality continues in the actual meeting, where it's key to address people by their correct title (say, 'Madame la Présidente') and in order of seniority. In fact, don't see it as failure if your business counterparts stick to 'Monsieur' and use the 'vous' type of address forever, rather than switching to first names, as this is seen as perfectly normal to maintain a healthy distance.
- Meetings should have a formal agenda and formal notes (a good thing in any case), which you can use to your advantage by referring back to an earlier decision made and documented in the 'meeting of the 13th of May', if necessary. This also helps to avoid the situation where you think your French counterpart has agreed to your investment proposal, but really they haven't and were only nodding out of politeness.

- The French working day starts and ends later, so a meeting before 10am is generally inadvisable as your counterpart will either decline or worse, turn up grumpy. Lunch is a very important time of day, so don't schedule a meeting for 1pm unless it's an actual lunch (and if you do, make it a nice one). On the other hand, 5pm or even 6pm meetings are potentially acceptable.
- Some older, more senior French executives don't speak English as well as you might expect — which they might not admit for fear of embarrassment. So, if you attend a meeting where a senior person does lots of nodding but not much talking, you'd better double check what they think they've agreed to.
- Better yet, try and speak a little French of your own — it goes a long way. However, unless you live in the country, it'll be a while until you can partake in an actual French conversation. The language is not only hard to learn but has an entire parallel universe of colloquial words — did you know a car is actually a 'caisse' or 'bagnole', shoes are 'pompes' or 'baskets' and clothes are 'fringues', to name but a few?
- Despite their sometime reputation to the contrary, most French work pretty hard and to a high standard: From any written piece of communication, they'll expect a crisp, logical line of reasoning as well as solid backup analysis.
- And finally, the French are very proud to be French so best not to make fun of their country or one of their companies as they're likely to

take it very personally. Find common ground in complaining about other nationalities instead.
- **Top Ice-Breaking Tip:** Talk about your favourite item of French cuisine.

THE ITALIANS

- Image is everything and that counts for both personal appearance (apparently, Italian gyms have changing rooms twice the size of English ones to accommodate more space for preening in front of giant mirrors) but also business transactions. So, dress well and avoid putting an Italian in a situation where they might lose face, particularly in front of colleagues.
- Expect Italians to be generally more direct in their interactions with you than French and Germans, so don't be surprised if you're told that your idea isn't particularly good. It normally comes from a desire to be honest and helpful rather than to be needlessly critical. It also comes from a love of talking so be prepared to simply nod and listen for quite some time.
- In fact, disagreements can quickly turn into heated arguments with a lot of hand-waving and the occasional raising of voices, which isn't necessarily a cause for alarm. On the flipside, Italians won't hold too much of a grudge, so if the shouting is followed by *aperitivo* drinks you're still in with a chance of success.
- Strangely enough, I've found Italians to be less proud of their country and their companies than really they should be — here is one of the few remaining European countries that thinks UK or

US companies are inherently likely to be better than Italian ones, so use it to your advantage.
- While hierarchical structures remain very important (and finding the right person to make a decision can be tricky), rules and regulations are at best a guideline and at worst irrelevant. This includes meeting start and end times, which are a general indication rather than a precise appointment.
- **Top Ice-Breaking Tip:** Start a conversation about a recent item of topical news.

THE SPANISH

- Very similar to Italians except with a little more pride in their country's organisations but perhaps a little more earnestness thrown in when it comes to business conversations. So, do your research not only on your counterpart but the Spanish business environment more generally.
- Everything is a little bit more relaxed than in Italy, with Spanish hosts particularly keen to ensure you have a great time when you visit and get to experience some of the local culture: "Yes I know you're very busy but we must have a coffee on the terrace first."
- While actual siestas are a thing of the past, generally life starts and ends even later than in Italy, with a dinner at 9pm considered relatively early. Hence, make sure your stamina is at its peak if you ever visit the country
- **Top Ice-Breaking Tip:** Compliment the Spanish climate and outdoorsy way of living.

THE GERMANS

- The Germans pretend that they're very different to the French but in many ways they're not — there's almost as much formality involved when it comes to meetings, both in terms of setup and execution, just with less good coffee and definitely no wine. So all the points about French meetings made above equally apply to German ones, except that their English is normally better and next steps are typically more straightforward to understand.
- Having said that, meeting formality appears to be changing somewhat. While older people remain attached to titles, formal invitations and so on, younger folk are keener to emulate Anglo-Saxon ways. So after a bit of ice-breaking, you're more likely to find someone willing to be more informal and potentially bend the rules a little bit, especially if they appear to be wearing fancy trainers. Come to think of it, this applies to the French as well, though perhaps not as much.
- Additionally, Germans are extremely proud of the quality of their products and processes, and can find excitement in the minutiae of even the most mundane products — be prepared for very detailed questions on anything you're presenting, particularly if it's remotely technical.
- When proposing a meeting time, remember to set your watch back two hours from 'French time' so that it becomes perfectly normal to hold a meeting

at 8am, whereas anything after 4pm is unlikely to be advisable as it will be almost time for dinner.
- And finally, just like in France it's unlikely you'll ever call someone by their first name in a business context. Stick to 'Herr Meier' and 'Frau Huber' plus the formal 'Sie' rather than 'Du' — the latter best reserved for any trips to the Austrian Alps (highly recommended in all seasons, but as an Austrian I'm biased!)
- **Top Ice-Breaking Tip:** Praise the craftsmanship of your counterpart's product

THE DUTCH

- The Dutch are really tall (which takes a while to get used to), very easy going but also very direct — shockingly so for someone used to working in England. Within an hour of my first meeting in Holland, with someone I hadn't met before, I was both told that my presentation was 'pretty bad' and asked how many children I had, very matter-of-factly. On the plus side, you'll know very quicky where you stand.
- Meetings start and end on time and responsibility is often delegated so you generally need to jump through fewer hoops to get decisions made, as even relatively junior people are empowered to crack on. And if they don't, they'll soon tell you.
- Food is really more of a rational affair so you don't need to worry about it too much and indeed may want to consider self-catering. The Dutch speak unnervingly good English (so don't bother learning

any Dutch) and many are aiming to be achingly cool although not everyone pulls this off entirely.
- **Top Ice-Breaking Tip:** Have a matter-of-fact conversation about your respective families.

THE BRITS

- Last but not least, the Brits! After over 25 years here, I feel like I've become 49% British (still 51% Austrian, though) but I'm happy to report that most of the stereotypes are indeed true for Brits just as much as for other nationalities. Awkward silences? Tick. Stiff upper lips? Tick. Bamboozling expressions? Tick. Keen on pubs? Also tick.
- On the plus side, you'll find a pretty friendly and straightforward environment with relatively little formality and most people quickly on first name terms. A little humour, preferably of the dry variety, also helps (perhaps watch Monty Python's 'Dead Parrot Sketch' in preparation).
- This also makes it quite easy to build relationships, assuming you're willing to put in the effort. The most important thing here is to always accept an invitation to lunch or the pub, which are likely to be quickly forthcoming. You'd be surprised how seamlessly you'll be included in the conversation if you're willing to give it a go.
- In meetings, it's customary to start with a little small talk before you get to the subject matter, stereotypically about the weather but anything anodyne will do: your travels to the meeting, a recent holiday or

what you had for breakfast. Don't however expect a deep conversation or even much of a response, as the small talk is there only to bridge the awkward silence before the meeting actually starts.
- The main thing to watch out for is that Brits have an amazing ability to not actually say what they really mean, use unusual expressions, or both. This can be confusing for both sides and lead to issues further down the road, so I've reproduced below a list of common misinterpretations to get you started — this is also important if you're a Brit because your foreign opposite number might actually expect an invitation to the lunch that you've promised them!
- **Top Ice-Breaking Tip:** Comment on the weather, or (if you know it) about your counterpart's favourite Premier League football team.

UNDERSTANDING PEOPLE (3): WHERE THEY'RE FROM

WHAT THE BRITISH SAY	WHAT THE BRITISH MEAN	WHAT OTHERS UNDERSTAND
I hear what you say	I disagree and do not want to discuss it further	He accepts my point of view
With the greatest respect...	I think you are an idiot	He is listening to me
That's not bad	That's good	That's poor
That is a very brave proposal	You are insane	He thinks I have courage
Quite good	A bit disappointing	Quite good
I would suggest...	Do it or be prepared to justify yourself	Think about the idea, but do what you like
Oh, incidentally / by the way	The primary purpose of our discussion is...	That is not very important
I was a bit disappointed that...	I am annoyed that...	It doesn't really matter
Very interesting	That is clearly nonsense	They are impressed
I'll bear it in mind	I've forgotten it already	They will probably do it
I'm sure it's my fault	It's your fault	Why do they think it was their fault?
You must come for dinner	It's not an invitation, I'm just being polite	I will get an invitation soon
I almost agree	I don't agree at all	He's not far from agreement
I only have a few minor comments	Please re-write completely	He has found a few typos
Could we consider some other options	I don't like your idea	They have not yet decided

I hope this was a mildly fun romp through some of the key European nationalities[16] you may encounter. Please do take it in the (light-hearted) spirit in which it was intended, although I'm also happy to receive angry correspondence on LinkedIn if you think I've got it wrong.

This brings me back to the London-Amsterdam route launch that I mentioned at the beginning of the chapter. One of my first objectives was to get the German train manufacturers to work together with the French timetablers and the Dutch security experts, as well as assorted Brits from my company. After much political horse-trading I managed to arrange a kick-off meeting in Amsterdam but I could sense there was still a reticence to engage, which I wanted to overcome. So I scheduled the meeting for 11am followed by lunch (still a good ice-breaker for all nationalities), but to make sure I'd warmed everyone up beforehand, I arranged to meet all three delegations privately, for breakfast. Which of course meant the Germans at 07:30, the Dutch at 08:30 and the French at 09:30, none of whom found that particular timing even remotely odd. The eventual meeting was a success, but I did find that third coffee and croissant rather tricky.

---

16 A test reader suggested expanding this chapter to include Americans, Chinese and others, but I don't feel as qualified to talk about non-Europeans and in any case the chapter was already long enough! Perhaps in the second edition.

ACTION

Identify a current or past project involving one or more people from a different nationality. How could you use (or have used) your understanding of cultural norms to improve your chances of success?

Managing your boss

Who's the best boss you've ever had? What about the worst one? And why did you pick those two characters? While unfortunately I can't hear your answers (I'd love to actually), I think that in the best management situations there's a sort of symbiotic relationship at play. You know, like those little oxpecker birds that sit on top of wildebeest or zebra — as the National History Museum says (David Attenborough voice optional), "The birds pick at parasites on the mammal's body, including ticks and blood-sucking flies. This may help keep the mammal's parasite load under control, and the birds get an easy meal."

Perhaps I'm pushing this analogy a bit far — I do eventually want you to become the zebra so if you're currently the little bird, then that's going to be tricky. However, the point is that management relationships should be two way streets where you manage your boss just as much as your boss manages you. Obviously, I know that hierarchically that isn't true and ultimately your boss is responsible for setting your goals and assessing the quality of your work, as well as putting you forward for promotions and pay rises. So I'm not suggesting you upend that principle and start telling your boss what to do. You will remain the 'direct report' and they will remain the 'line manager', strictly speaking (although perhaps later in life you could leapfrog them, which would be nice if slightly awkward).

However, what I am suggesting is that you apply the principles outlined above on understanding motivations and incentives even more to your boss than to your other colleagues. Precisely because they have so much power over you, they need to be the person you understand the best. Use all the levers described earlier, including the one-to-one sessions you hopefully have with them regularly, to really get under their skin so that eventually you know how they'll react even before they do.

This is important for a number of reasons. Firstly, it gives you a much better chance of having an 'adult to adult' relationship with your boss based on trust and mutual understanding, as opposed to a 'parent-child' relationship based on a top-down power dynamic. Without wanting to delve too deeply into this bit of psychology developed by Eric Berne in the 1950s under the title 'Transactional Analysis'[17], the parent-child dynamic can quickly become suffocating and is unlikely to allow you much room for growth. Maybe that's OK early on in a role or if your boss is very senior and for a while you're just happy to take orders and learn, but soon enough you'll need to become an 'adult' yourself if you'd like to progress up the ladder.

Secondly, it's almost always in your interest to *make your boss look good* to the wider organisation (and externally) and that's a lot easier if you understand them well and can therefore prevent any mistakes or awkward moments before they happen (or at minimum, not make things worse). Generally,

---

17 For more information, see Further Reading

bosses have fragile egos so if you can bolster that ego rather than bruise it, it's likely that they'll repay you by giving you more trust and responsibility going forward. Like it or not, this also includes accepting that they'll occasionally take one of your ideas and repackage it as their own. REALLY frustrating, I know (how very dare they!), but consider whether the end justifies the means — if you get your proposal approved, your project funded and some extra boss-creds, does it really matter if they stole your idea?

Of course, staying in the shadows isn't always the right answer and occasionally, leaning in more strongly and potentially upstaging your boss in front of more senior people is the right thing to do, to prove that you're ready for bigger and better things. However, it may quickly lead to a permanent rift, so be very careful what you wish for. More often, it's better to win as a team so that both of you go places together, at least for a while.

Finally, if you understand your boss well, it'll make it much easier to push their buttons so that they do what's best for you when it really matters. Doing a fabulous job and hitting all your targets is great, but it's unlikely on its own to be sufficient to get that project or promotion you really wanted. Like it or not, your boss is normally the best person to make these things happen for you, so knowing them well allows you to give your boss feedback that they might actually act upon. If they're numbers driven then give them numbers, even if that doesn't make much sense in the circumstances. If they're ideas-driven, give them ideas! I know this can be tricky if your boss has a very different approach from your own. If this applies to you, swallow your pride and use the in-depth knowledge of your boss as an advantage to get what you want.

This isn't to say that understanding your boss is easy — sometimes it is, but sometimes bosses intentionally keep at a distance from their team, at least on a personal level, making it hard to build a good relationship. Or they're intentionally unreasonable in their asks, just to see how far they can push you. Unfortunately there is no magic solution here and your only option is to keep trying, and to force the conversation even when this might be uncomfortable. Perhaps you can tag-team with your peers to solve the problem together?

This brings me back to the best and worst bosses I asked you about at the beginning. While some bosses are inherently better than others, it's likely that the 'bad' bosses just have a very different way of operating than you do. And unless you manage to find a way to change boss (which in more extreme circumstances should definitely be an option), you're stuck with them for a while, whether you like it or not. So don't spend your time complaining, as great as that may feel, but instead use their motivations and incentives to your advantage. That way, you can turn most bad bosses into reasonable ones — or at least avoid them doing you any harm.

ACTION

Create two columns, one labelled 'what engages my boss' and the other 'what doesn't'. Complete as much of both sides as you can, based on your interactions so far. It doesn't have to be very structured and can be a mixture of ways of communicating ('quick answers on Slack'), types of outputs ('the weekly revenue report') and things outside of work ('oat lattes', 'Crystal Palace FC') — or indeed anything else that comes to mind. Then, identify a desired outcome (an investment, a decision) that your boss has so far blocked. Use your learnings above to draw up an action plan: what new ways could you use to convince your boss to say yes?

Making people feel special: Free fries in Greece

One summer I was lucky enough to stay in a lovely mountain resort on the Greek island of Crete. Beautiful little villas were clustered around a communal area featuring a swimming pool, some classic summer activities such as table tennis, and a taverna for breakfasts and dinners. A multitude of terraces offered sweeping views over the Cretan hills and a hidden orchestra of cicadas supplied the musical accompaniment. It was nothing very fancy, but a wonderfully relaxing place to spend a few days with my family.

The resort was owned and run by Manolis, a deceptively quiet forty-something who turned out to be the most consummate hotelier I have ever seen. Of course, he was personable, friendly and accommodating, as you would hope the owner of a 'boutique' hotel to be. But more than that, he had an incredible knack for making people feel special, by spending a little time with each of them and then giving them exactly what they were looking for. Achieving this with every one of fifty guests at the same time is arguably a contradiction in terms — surely if everyone is special, then no one is. Yet, Manolis deftly pulled it off with the skills of a wizard. He had run his hotel for over 20 years, but it was nonetheless impressive.

MAKING PEOPLE FEEL SPECIAL: FREE FRIES IN GREECE

For me, it all started with a passing mention that I was keen to climb Crete's highest mountain, located not far away from the resort. Manolis didn't say much at the time, but the next day quietly pulled me aside after breakfast to show me a detailed trail map of the area: "I knew I had it somewhere, but it took me a while to find it for you". He then proceeded to explain, in detail, the various available options with associated pros and cons. But his *pièce de resistance* came at dinner that night, when my hungry children had finished their portion of French fries and were slightly forlornly licking the last drops of ketchup off their empty plate. When Manolis noticed this, he sidled up to them and said in a loud whisper, "would you like some extra fries for free"?

If you have children, you'll be able to imagine what effect these words had on my two. If you don't, please picture yourself being pulled aside at the gate of your transatlantic flight, to be given a free upgrade to business class — it's roughly the same. Except that the cost of extra fries is less than £1, whereas my children are already badgering me to return — a very impressive ROI indeed.

Manolis was so masterful at this game that for the first two days I thought that only my family were on the receiving end of his generosity — the quintessence of feeling special, of course. It required astute observation to discover that he applied his technique to everyone — be it to set up a more secluded table for a romantic couple, prepare a takeaway breakfast for early risers, or find the right food for picky toddlers. Eventually it became mesmerising to observe him in full flow; a little like watching a painter conjure a landscape out of thin air, or a chef making a soufflé. And Manolis didn't limit his magic to his customers: he could sometimes be seen plating food in the kitchen at the height of dinner service while having a little chat with chef, and his staff looked all the happier for it.

Of course, Manolis isn't the only one who uses personal attention as a way to engage customers and staff. Pret gives the occasional free coffee, airlines have created entire experiences for premium customers and the number of employee awards, big and small, seems to be multiplying. And that's because making people feel special is a very powerful tool, not just for the here and now (when you need something in return straight away) but more importantly as a bank of goodwill to dip into sometime in the future. Not to mention that it feels great to cheer someone up.

In a work context, this technique is particularly effective with more junior people who might not otherwise get a huge amount of attention, but from whom you may well need help later. Indeed, the CEO and the executive team will be sweet-talked all the time and may start feeling slightly wary about it — "stop asking me about my family and just tell me what you want...", though that shouldn't stop you from trying in the appropriate way. The CEO's assistant, on the other hand, may be more used to being taken for granted or worse, complained to when the CEO once again cancels a meeting. Ditto the receptionist, often ignored until the printer stops working or a parcel gets delivered. Members of the IT team (whom you'll eventually need to fix your computer), data analysts (who can help you answer that all-important analytical question), financial controllers (useful to have suppliers paid or expenses approved), junior lawyers (who can gain or

MAKING PEOPLE FEEL SPECIAL: FREE FRIES IN GREECE

lose precious days on your contracts), the list is endless. You'll probably get your work done eventually if you treat them as transactional cogs in the system, but if you make them feel special, everything will be a lot smoother, better quality, and more fun too.

The good news is that this isn't very hard, partly because so few people do it (despite the obvious pay-offs) and partly because if you try *too* hard it'll come across as a bit weird and, well, trying too hard. It can be as simple as saying hello and smiling, helping out occasionally, listening to people's concerns, spending a couple of minutes longer talking to them than strictly necessary, or just making them a cup of tea (remembering they only want a splash of milk but two sugars). It doesn't have to cost much or take a lot of time, but if you manage to make people feel special, it will pay dividends many times over. And as a bonus, it's also a lovely two-way dopamine hit where the recipient's positive reaction feeds back onto you: they're happy, you're happy, and you've banked some capital for the future. Win-win.

PS: I do heartily recommend staying with Manolis. You can find him on eleonas.gr

ACTION

Pick two people in your organisation with whom you'd like to build a better relationship by making them feel special. Ideally, pick people who you think might be useful to you in future, but who also seem intrinsically interesting so you can have a genuine conversation. Then make a mini plan on how to approach them, bearing in mind that it should feel natural to both of you (and create a nice interaction full stop) rather than, say, you awkwardly handing flowers to someone you've never met!

Working with idiots

An immutable fact of working life is that every company has a few idiots that you'd rather didn't exist. You know the ones you tell your partner about when you come home in the evening, or when you leave in the morning. "I have a meeting with Bruce today", you'll say over breakfast, sighing heavily and prompting a sympathetic look. While your partner still doesn't quite know what you actually do all day, they sure know Bruce and the fact that he is really very annoying.

Now when I say *idiots*, I don't actually mean just stupid people in the classic sense of the word (i.e., those who just aren't quite with the programme). I'm actually applying a very loose definition here of basically anyone at work whom you just find plain irritating. This could be for a whole host of reasons, some of them rational (they messed you around once) and some of them not (they just make this really annoying sound when they eat).

ACTION 1

Start by making a mental list of who would fall in that category in your current organisation. You could write down their names below, although you never know who might end up picking up this book in future! If it makes you feel better, use this time to briefly reminisce about idiots you worked with in previous companies but have now left behind, particularly those that have since had some sort of comeuppance.

How many names are on your list? I'm very much hoping it's only a handful because if we're reaching double digits or you've just written down ALL OF THEM, then this chapter alone is unlikely to make much of a difference and you should look for a different job instead. Let's proceed on the assumption that your list has something like three to five people, which I think is a reasonable expectation given that the biggest idiots are likely to take up a disproportionate part of your mindspace.

Now, what are we going to do about the people on your list? Here's a controversial suggestion to begin with: I'm going to bet that actually, not all of your idiots are really idiots. This is partly because I believe that most people are basically good (and you should give them a chance) and partly because there may be an explanation for their behaviour, such as:

- Maybe you're on the opposite end of the colour axes described earlier

- Maybe they're just stressed, who knows what they're going through at home

- Maybe they're just generally a bit insecure about their job or their boss or they have impostor syndrome (it happens to us all sometimes)

- Maybe you did something to trigger them. Be honest now, we're all idiots sometimes

- Or maybe you've just jumped to a conclusion based on your early interactions and haven't really given them a chance since

ACTION 2

Take each person in turn and describe why they're an idiot. What have they actually done to be so harshly classified? Do they do this regularly or have they done it just the once? Then think long and hard about why they might be exhibiting this behaviour. Try to be charitable and assume the best rather than the worst.

If you think that's tricky, then the next bit is even harder: I want you to test your hypothesis by *actually talking to the person in question*. "What? Talk to *Bruce*?" I hear you scream in agony but yes, that is indeed what I'm suggesting. You need a bit of a game plan here, otherwise it'll be really awkward really quickly, but I'd like you to try. Take them out for coffee, grab them at the end of a meeting, pull them aside at the summer party; I don't care how you do it, but give it a go. "Hey Bruce, you know when you said XYZ last week, I didn't quite understand why you would do that..." or even better, "Hey Bruce, I wonder if my presentation the other week upset you because..." You never know, you might even end up making a new friend in the process.

If you truly can't face talking to them directly then you do have a couple of alternatives. You could check in with someone you trust, but make sure you have an honest conversation rather than asking them to confirm your judgment. Or just observe the person more closely for a few days to see if your theory holds. Maybe they only react to certain comments or certain people? Maybe not everything they do is idiotic? But watch out for *confirmation bias* (where you just interpret people's actions in the way that confirms what you already assumed).

Now review your list: Let's say there are two or three people left who are the truly annoying ones, and that won't change whatever you do[18]. How do you deal with them? You're left with the following options:

---

18 I'm convinced that more often than not this comes from a deep insecurity somewhere, so maybe have a little sympathy for them even if they drive you up the wall.

- The easiest way to deal with true idiots is to just have as little to do with them as humanly possible. Find ways to avoid meetings with them, say hi but keep walking in the corridor, and certainly don't get involved in Slack or email threads. You might even find that the feeling is mutual and your target is quite happy with this arrangement because they've also spent their evenings talking to their partners about you!

- Alternatively, or in addition, make a deal with them whereby you won't get in their way and they won't get in yours. Of course, doing a deal with the devil can go spectacularly wrong so only do it with your eyes wide open. But you might just find that working together (potentially against a common enemy who's even worse, or to achieve a goal like extra funding) beats working against each other.

- And then there is the nuclear option: Build a coalition of like-minded people against your idiot, potentially involving HR. This may sound like an attractive choice because of the sheer satisfaction you'll derive, but make no mistake, it's high risk. No one likes idiots but no one likes backstabbers either.

- You could of course just be an idiot back to them, but we all know where that ends so while you may consider it for a minute, please don't. It's just not worth it.

When I spoke to people about writing this book, this chapter was invariably the one that elicited a lot of interest, which I assume proves that we all have to work with idiots occasionally.

But maybe sometimes we're not helping ourselves and in any case understanding other people's motivations is always a good idea. And in my experience, the proper idiots will get found out eventually so in the meantime, you can sit on your high horse of moral superiority.

ACTION 3

Make a plan for how to deal with each of your remaining targets, based on the options provided above.

Active listening: An endangered skill worth honing

As I sit at my kitchen table writing this book on my laptop, I'm lucky enough to have my wife next to me doing her own work on her own laptop. For a few precious months, I'm a full-time author so I get to have lunch with her most days, sometimes out in the garden. We take it in turns to prepare our twice-daily coffees and keep supplies of tea topped up (peppermint for me, Earl Grey for her). Very idyllic so far but there's a serious point coming soon.

Occasionally, I get to a natural break in proceedings where I could really do with some advice on a point in the book, or it just helps to repeat it out loud. "Hey Abi, do you think a chapter on active listening would be a good end to the people section? I'm not sure I have a good example to build on yet." Abi, who runs a manufacturing business, is fully focused on doing payroll or sourcing obscure ingredients from faraway places. After a moment, she might say, "sounds good", followed by, "but you should really hire someone to publicise your book". To which I might reply, "and what about my idea for the epilogue"?

We may be worse than other couples in terms of paying proper attention to each other, but I doubt it — I reckon it's a microcosm of the slow but steady decline of what psychologists call 'active listening', defined as paying full attention to a speaker's words and emotions with the aim to truly understand. This isn't limited to the home, it's just as much an issue in the workplace. With a hundred objectives for the day and limited opportunities for proper conversation, who's got the time? And yet, active listening improves communication and enhances understanding, ultimately leading to stronger, more meaningful relationships. As a positive side effect, it also allows all ideas to be heard rather than the dominant person in the room carrying the conversation.

There are two steps to active listening: First, don't be distracted and focus on your conversation with the other person. That should be the easy bit but with so many things on our minds and so many devices calling for our attention, it's not always a given. Second, *actually* listen to what the other person is saying to you, as opposed to focusing on the point that you want to make next. That bit is even harder — clever person that you are, when someone speaks for more than 30 seconds you might soon have one of two reactions: 1) *I already know what you're saying, so I don't have the patience to listen* or 2) *I don't agree with what you're saying, so I'm already focusing on my response.* Or possibly even 3) *I wasn't listening in the first place, because I'm just here to make a point.* None of which will make you actively listen, and all of which are likely to annoy your opposite number.

The good news is that active listening is a skill that you can practice like any other. For a start, force yourself to take a deep breath while the other person is talking and actually let them finish their sentence rather than barging in. Then, repeat back roughly the point the other person made or clarify what they've said so you definitely understand ("what I'm hearing is..."), although beware of using this as an excuse to add your own interpretation. Finally, ask open questions to encourage them to elaborate.

To be clear, I'm not saying that you need to become Confucius, stroking your metaphorical beard while patiently listening to all and sundry, only to occasionally utter a deeply meaningful phrase. Many conversations will be more transactional, and you will need to find a balance between listening and speaking in time-constrained situations, which won't be easy. However, taking the time to actively listen when it really matters, at least for a short period, is key to working well with other people. Indeed, possibly more so because in busy or tense situations and if you're a confident person, it's just too easy to fall back into your standard way of operating — to stop listening and focus on what you've got to say at the expense of what others are saying to you. (And thank you for asking, but Abi and I have been together for 30 years and are aiming for another 50 if we're lucky!)

ACTION

Reflect for a minute on your current active listening skills and give yourself an honest grade out of ten. Then write down an example of where you've done it well, and one where you haven't. Finally, pick an upcoming meeting where you'll try and do it better, writing down a few ideas on how you'll achieve it.

PART 4

HOW TO BE GOOD AT YOUR JOB (ADVANCED)

What did you think of that last section? Did I promise too much? I do hope that even if you're an introvert / misanthrope / emotionally stilted, I at least showed you the power of working well with other people. In all stages of your career, but especially as you get more senior, you won't be able to get much done without the help of others, so whether you like it or not, understanding people is key to moderate success — perhaps more so than any other skill.

Having said that, let's now come back to a more self-centred section on how to do well at your job. Here, we'll focus on advanced skills, which you're more likely to need in slightly more senior, mid-management roles — such as setting priorities and goals, making decisions, problem-solving and negotiating. We'll also have a short section specifically on managing people, which you're likely to start doing once you reach a certain level (and takes us back again to working with other people, except this time they're 'your people').

There's also a chapter on using humour in the workplace, just to add a bit of (serious) fun.

As always you're welcome to read the chapters in the order they're presented or jump straight into a topic that you find particularly interesting. You're making great progress, so keep going!

Strategy is deciding what not to do

It's early July and together with the other top 20 executives of my company, I've decamped to a nice country house hotel near London for a couple of days. The weather is pleasant, the birds are singing and we're sitting in a semi-circle about to share a personal anecdote, to build better relationships as a team. Welcome to the start of the annual strategy planning cycle, which will run until January and involve untold meetings, presentations and spreadsheets to help us set our priorities for the coming year.

It's a well-intentioned and often very interesting process where we'll review the priority level of existing workstreams (should we dial up or down the investment in the international business, for example) as well as looking at the wider market environment to see what new opportunities (such as deregulation) and threats (like new competitors) may lurk on the horizon. (As an aside, a rough effort split of 70%/20%/10% between existing work, known new opportunities and speculative new opportunities is a good benchmark to shoot for.)

It is however also a pretty painful process of ever more detailed meetings that drag on over months, finishing with sometimes undignified haggling over the last remaining resources and the associated financial targets that are the basis for next year's budget. At the end, it still feels like we've fudged some of the big decisions in favour of trying to be all things to all people and not making anyone feel left out.

This isn't because the whole thing is badly run. Everyone is trying to do their best, discussions are open and there are thankfully few political shenanigans. No, it's because at the heart of it, setting strategic priorities is *deciding what not to do*. And that is really hard because it involves saying No to things that are perfectly good ideas — actively cutting off some sources of revenue to double down on fewer, bigger bets.

This isn't just the case for annual strategy plans, it also holds true for all prioritisation processes, including those within your control. At any one time, in most companies it's likely that you have too many interesting topics clamouring for your attention. Using a basic 2x2 matrix of effort versus reward, some of these will be easy to agree on — low effort, high reward, what's not to like. Others will be easy to dismiss: high effort, low reward, don't bother. But normally that still leaves you with way too many potentially sensible topics to which you could allocate your time and money.

So you have to find a way to prioritise, and I'm sorry to say that doing a little bit of everything is never the right answer. Yes, it might feel most comfortable because it means you don't have to disappoint anyone and you don't have to forgo any revenue sources, however small. Sure, you could increase revenue from say Portugal by 10% if you spent a bit of time on it, but that only increases overall revenue by 0.1%. Using that same effort on developing your new product line might mean it actually sees the light of day much faster, giving you a chance of a 5% increase to sales next year. It can be a gut-wrenching decision because your Portuguese country manager is likely to be disappointed and you're choosing to leave revenue on the table today. But it'll pay off in the long run and provides clarity and focus to teams in the short term. You need to be quite ruthless here — don't fall into the temptation to fudge it, but truly say no to some things! In my experience, you can anyway really only focus on two or three big activities every quarter (plus perhaps a few smaller ones).

Of course, it's not enough simply to decide what your priorities are — what you're not going to be working on. That's only half the job done. The other half is to make sure you've communicated your decisions to all and sundry. Then to communicate it again. And then to communicate it again and again. Companies tend to be like cruise ships, they move quite fast but they turn very slowly, so don't expect everyone to remember your priorities and act accordingly just because you've sent them an email or put the information up on the office wall. Instead, repeat your strategy at every possible opportunity until you're sick of hearing yourself talk about it. At that point you might be starting to achieve some cut-through.

The other thing to remember is that prioritisation isn't a one-off exercise, but like an apple tree its smaller branches need to be regularly pruned so that the larger ones have a chance to fully develop and grow some juicy fruit. When a new business opportunity appears, it can be easy enough (and exciting) to jump on it — "Germany has opened up as a market, we've got to get a taskforce going straight away"! And that may well be the right thing to do, but just as starting up the new workstream is important, so is deciding what will be stopped to make room. Companies are great at adding new objectives but terrible at taking the old ones away, so you need to be extra vigilant here.

Next time you complain about your manager or the company as a whole making a prioritisation decision with which you disagree, bear in mind that they might well be doing you a favour by providing focus — if nobody's upset by the company strategy, then it's likely to be so bland and all-encompassing that it's not really a strategy at all. It needs to be the same for the work that you and your team do: To be most effective, what you say No to is way more important than what you say Yes to; and if it doesn't hurt a little bit somewhere, then really you haven't made big enough decisions. Hey, I never said that the road to moderate success was going to be easy!

ACTION

Make a list of all the major activities that you or your team are currently working on. You don't have to include really tiny pieces of work but I'd expect the list to have somewhere between 5 to 15 entries.

Next, pick at least one of those activities — preferably two or three — that you'll stop doing until further notice. Actively decide where to put the resources that you've freed up, although one of the options may just be on more leisure time! Then, make yourself a plan on how to communicate your decision: who needs to know and what is your reasoning? Depending on your situation, you may need to enlist the help of your manager for additional buy-in and air cover.

Setting goals: Aboard the riverboat *Steam Queen*

A while back I was travelling with some family and friends on a lovely boat on the River Thames called the *Steam Queen*. It was one of these perfect-for-boating days when the sun is warm and the wind just strong enough to make your hair flutter without overly messing it up, so to celebrate the occasion I had bought a round of drinks from the downstairs bar. Unfortunately, my little bubble of perfection burst when I realised back on deck that I'd forgotten my daughter's lemonade, so I returned only to be informed that I couldn't buy *just* the £2 lemonade because of the £5 minimum spend for card payments, you see.

Now, if you have children you'll know that returning without the lemonade wasn't an option. Of course, I could have just bought a couple more drinks that I didn't need, but my rational response was to plead with the onboard staff to simply accept my card for the lower amount, as a) I'd already spent significantly more than the minimum overall, and b) the cost to the company of accepting my debit card would be pennies.

This is where it gets (mildly) interesting. The staff member (let's call him Rick), while very apologetic, said that he couldn't possibly do that because his boss had told him in no uncertain terms that he'd had enough of people flouting the payment rules and would be spot checking the receipts to make sure. Rick liked his job more than he liked me, so understandably wasn't prepared to take this risk.

Now, I don't much like taking No for an answer and was steeling myself to explain the flaws in this logic when Rick turned back to me and said "you know what though, you can just have the drink for free if you like. That wouldn't be a problem for me."

For Rick, this made perfect sense. Boss *really cares* about minimum payment, so I can't break that. However, Boss *doesn't much care* about stock levels, so I can do what I like. But for the company, it makes no sense. The exchange has left it £1.90 out of pocket. Having really tight control in one area may make Boss feel good, but just like steam escaping through a different vent, it's likely those pesky employees will come up with an alternative (and possibly worse) way to solve their problems.

The lemonade example is of course trivial, but the world is full of rules with unintended consequences, and this is just as true of company goals and targets. In most cases, the initial thought was probably sound, but the problem is that human beings respond extraordinarily well to incentives, especially so if they're linked to tangible rewards or sanctions, so you need to be careful what you wish for. To be clear, I'm not saying that you shouldn't try and set measurable goals: countless studies have shown that companies with clear goals are more successful than those without. You just need to find the right balance between holding people to account but not slavishly sticking to something that doesn't make sense.

This is easier said than done, and in my experience companies can spend months debating the right goals and still get it wrong. So how do you set good goals? You might have heard of the SMART methodology (specific — measurable — actionable — results-oriented — time-bound), which is a good starting point. But I find it a bit narrow, so here's a slightly more extensive list of what, in my view, makes a good goal:

- It should be clearly linked to overall departmental or company objectives, so that everyone knows how their work contributes to company success. For example, an improvement to customer experience should link into an overall customer satisfaction target.

- The goal should not only be measurable, but there needs to be reasonable certainty that its achievement is linked to the actions of the people responsible. If the goal is driven by many factors (including external ones), it's unlikely to be very useful. For example, overall conversion rate is usually a terrible goal because it depends on so many factors, making it very difficult to pinpoint specific drivers.

- Nonetheless, it needs to be simple enough to understand — if you need a two-page explainer of how it's calculated, try again.

- The goal should be motivating to your team in and of itself. 'Increase revenue by 20%' is rarely something that gets people excited, so find something more engaging. For example, 'sell 100,000 discount cards' worked great in a recent role because we hadn't even sold 20,000 when we started, so it was something that the whole team could rally around.

- Finally, keep the number of goals manageable so that people can remember them and they provide sufficient focus and clarity. I'd suggest either three or five, but not four because — I'm not sure why — it really does feel strange to have even-numbered lists.

Goal setting is far from straightforward, balancing as it does the needs to be simple yet precise, stretchy yet achievable and motivating yet measurable. However, setting good goals — and avoiding perverse incentives in the process — is crucial to company success and employee engagement, so make sure you spend the required time getting it right.

ACTION

Take your or your team's goals for the current period. Review them against the criteria described above and most importantly, check that they actually make sense! If necessary, find a way to change those goals that are sub-optimal.

Solving problems: The hypothesis-based approach

Imagine you've agreed to have dinner with a friend of yours, and she asks where you'd like to go: you might struggle to answer because there's so much choice that you can't pick. But what if your friend suggests a Chinese restaurant? You don't like Chinese so you quickly point this out and instead suggest a Thai place in town, which you've been meaning to visit for ages. Now imagine being asked to write a presentation for an upcoming business meeting: you might sit for a while staring at an empty screen because you can't decide where to start or how to organise your thoughts. But what if a colleague asks you to comment on their draft version? I bet it'll take you fewer than five minutes to point out the flaws in their argument and suggest a couple of extra slides for inclusion.

These are small illustrations of the fact that it's generally much easier to comment on someone else's ideas than to come up with your own. I'm not exactly sure why, but maybe it's because you're worried about looking stupid by committing yourself to the 'wrong' answer. As people are generally not shy in providing criticism, it takes a brave person to stick their neck out with a solution they're not certain about. Ergo, you can waste a lot of time looking for the perfect answer pearl in the many shells of information. (Not my best-ever metaphor, I'll grant you.) What to do?

The answer is to turn problem solving on its head to start with a possible answer and then find the data to support it — rather than using the data to find the answer in the first place. In my strategy consulting days we used to call this 'hypothesis-based thinking' and the key to success is that to a certain degree, it doesn't matter whether your answer is right or wrong initially, because the process will flush this out. Let's say you're trying to decide what price to charge for a new product, but despite having done some research you can't settle on a final answer because there are so many variables. Rather than delaying the decision, pick one of the options as your preferred one and start getting feedback from the organisation or from customers. Fairly soon, you'll get an idea of the feasibility of this particular price and its advantages and downsides, allowing you to move forward with it, choose a different answer or perhaps obtain further data to make the decision — but you'll have sped up the process significantly.

In strategy consulting where time is often of the essence, we sometimes adopted an extreme version of this approach by writing the final presentation of a three-month project in its first week, calling it the 'Day 1 answer'. Doing so seemed insane because of how little we knew about the problem at hand, but it allowed us to focus our efforts on proving or disproving our initial hypotheses — a big time saver. Rather than looking for those elusive pearls in *all* the data, we could direct our searches quite precisely and ask: What would the data have to say for this hypothesis to be true? Allowing either more precise analysis or a targeted request for additional information rather than 'boiling the ocean'.

As a bonus, the method can be used to create buy-in within your organisation by presenting hypotheses as work in progress on which you're seeking your colleagues' input. Rather than stewing for a month and then presenting your answer as a fait accompli, you frame your thinking as co-creation: "Here's my thinking to date but I know it needs some further work, do you think I'm on the right track or am I missing something...?" Given enough time you can even pick up the same conversation later on and show your opposite number specifically how you've included their thinking in your work, creating further goodwill: "I've amended page 8 to include your comments from last time..."

While this method can be very effective, it's not without risks, principally two of them. First, you have to be clear that your hypotheses are only that — hypotheses. Don't believe in your infallibility and think that you know the final answer from the start, because people will realise that you're not really asking for their opinion and more importantly, because you're likely to be wrong. Always stay humble and be prepared to refine your thinking as you learn more. Second, even if you have the best intentions, not everyone in the organisation will be comfortable with considering hypotheses that could fundamentally alter their way of working. "What if we cut our salesforce in half?" might well be a fair hypothesis to test, but it's likely to cause an emotional reaction with many people — so you might want to present it a little less directly.

The hypothesis-based methodology is not only useful for big decisions such as strategic reviews or investments. The approach can also be used to extract information where none is forthcoming, as I discovered in my early days as a consultant when my role was often to do just that. Some of it was easy, because I was asking for ready-made data, but sometimes it was difficult as people were expected to give their judgment on a situation, which made them uncomfortable. One day I was sat in front of a production manager at a contact lens plant to understand how much time her team spent filling in paperwork. Asking her this question directly, I got a shrug accompanied by "je ne sais pas[19]" (this was in France). So I needed to change tack and go with "well, is it closer to 10% of your time or 50%?", which prompted the immediate reply of "it's definitely a lot more than 10%"! The initial barrier having been broken, we were off on a haggling discussion and eventually settled on around 25%.

Having thought about it some more, it's really the urge to disagree with a hypothesis that drives much of the value of this approach. Reluctant as we may be to offer our own view of things, we're certainly not shy in pointing out the flaws in that of others. So the sooner you understand that sticking your neck out and getting some flak for your views is actually a sensible way to get to a good answer, the faster you'll get there.

---

19 *I don't know*

ACTION

Pick a couple of problems where you are making slower progress than you would have liked, specifically because you can't decide what to do. For each of these:

- First, write down the first possible answer to your problem or decision that comes to mind. Crucially, it doesn't matter if it's the right answer. It doesn't even matter if it's a possible answer. All that matters is that you've written something down.

- Then, figure out how you can gather data to decide whether your answer is indeed correct. From whom can you get feedback? Are there any data that would help? What would you have to believe for it to be true?

- Finally, make a little plan on how to actually do these things in the next few days.

SOLVING PROBLEMS: THE HYPOTHESIS-BASED APPROACH

Making decisions: You don't always need to 'sleep on it'

One of my favourite hobbies is travel and within that, I'm mildly embarrassed to say, flying. Ever since I was a small kid I've loved the sense of wonder from sitting on a plane and looking down at the clouds; perusing the departure board at Heathrow still gives me goosebumps today, thinking of all those places I might visit.

It's fair to say however that what I enjoy even more than the travelling itself is the planning of said travelling. I'm not just talking about the standard decision of whether a Heathrow flight at 8am is worth the extra £50 compared to a Gatwick flight at 7am (it usually is). No, for a true flight geek like me that's way too simple a question and one that misses all the nuances that are vital to making the decision on what to book. What about the average punctuality of each flight? The type of aeroplane? The onboard seating? The likely security queue? The possibility of lounge access? The onboard food? The number of similarly-timed arrivals at the other end? And that's only the start. I'll happily disappear into my own world and will emerge with a colour coded spreadsheet a few days later, to proudly unveil to my family for the purposes of drawn-out discussion. At which point, they'll all look at me slightly bemused and say, "whatever, really. As long as we don't need to get up too early." And there you have it. A week's research meets with a collective shrug and I'm left to my own devices as to how to fine-tune the weight of each criterion in my spreadsheet. And as soon as my decision is finally made, I'll waste even more time on questioning whether it was in fact the correct one.

While this may be an extreme scenario, I'm consistently amazed by how much time is wasted on unimportant decision-making at work too. This is because decision-making time is usually driven not by how *important* the decision is but how *hard* it is to decide, because people are generally scared of *making the wrong decision*. So, an important but obvious call (such as which supplier to use if one of them is by far the best) may be made quite quickly, whereas a trivial but hard-to-agree one (say, which image to pick for a certain part of the website) can take forever. Yet, this lack of decision-making can waste untold hours not only weighing up the options but also holding up downstream work and letting confusion reign in the organisation. It may not be very much each time, but it soon adds up.

Therefore, you can unlock potentially huge productivity gains by speeding up decision-making, and not only on trivial items. To help, here's a handy decision-making checklist to get you on your way:

How important is this decision, really?
Be honest with yourself here, and think about the impact on your organisation rather than your personal view. How different are the proposed options in practice? What is the likely financial impact of making the 'wrong' decision? Will

the impact be measurable? Who will even notice? Particularly if you're a manager, you'll be surprised at how much time your team is spending on decisions that you think could be taken very quickly. Thinking is good, overthinking is not! Of course, some decisions will have a major impact but the choice of restaurant for your team Christmas dinner and the title of each individual slide are not among those.

Is it a two-way door?
Some decisions are permanent or at least long lasting — once you've chosen a new database, you're unlikely to change it soon — but many are not, so if your decision is reversible easily enough (a 'two-way door') then the risk of getting it wrong is reduced and you should feel more confident in getting on with it.

How much better will a detailed answer be vs. an 80/20 view?
Sure, some decisions require complex spreadsheets with multiple weighted criteria but many don't, because the answer is so obvious that it's staring you in the face. While I'm not advocating that you just make decisions on a whim the whole time, often a quick back of the envelope calculation will confirm your hunch and a much longer version of the same calculation won't change the outcome. The more senior you get, the more you should trust your gut feeling, augmented with a few useful data points — without becoming too complacent.

Will any new information come to light?
By now, you should have made those decisions that are either unimportant, can be easily reversed or where an 80% answer is good enough — I'd expect this to cover at least half of the

calls that you make. However, you're still left with some of the harder decisions that are important to get right. Surely, it's OK to spend some quality time on those? To 'sleep on it' a few more times? Well actually, it depends on whether any new information will come to light, or whether you already have all the data available to make your decision.

If it's the latter, then delaying the decision to next week is really just procrastination — your tough decision won't become any easier and all you'll do in the meantime is allow uncertainty to spread. If, having reviewed all the information, the right answer is that a member of your team needs to leave the organisation, then start the process today so that you can get it over and done with. Yes, it won't be pleasant, but it's not going to be any more pleasant in a week's time.

If of course you do need more information, then by all means delay your decision until you have all the facts and potentially get a wider range of views from across the business. However, make sure it's not just another excuse to avoid making a difficult decision (beloved by bosses, "thanks Matthias, this is helpful, but if you could just do that one last analysis for me...") and be honest with yourself about whether this new piece of information will make an actual difference.

In conclusion

Making decisions can be uncomfortable and sometimes scary. Not all consequences will be known and no one likes to be the person that makes the wrong call. But if decisions were easy then no one would need clever people like you to make them — they'd just be obvious. And the impact of not making a decision can often be bigger than that of making the wrong decision — projects get delayed, teams lack clarity and problems start building up. So face it: the more senior you become, the more your job is to muster your confidence, stick your neck out and get on with it! As a manager once said to me, "the key to being effective is to ask probing questions and every now and then, to make a decision."

ACTION

Identify a decision under your control that you've delayed making, perhaps because you were worried that you might pick the wrong answer. Use the questions above to decide how to speed up decision making and either make the decision then and there, or alternatively write down the additional information that you need to obtain. If there are negative consequences to your decision, accept those won't become easier with a delay and instead work up an action plan on how to mitigate them. Under no circumstances decide to 'sleep on it' one more time!

A Brief Interlude on humour

Having grown up in Austria, one of the earliest things I remember appreciating about the UK was its dry wit, as expressed by shows such as 'Monty Python's Flying Circus' and 'Fawlty Towers', and later 'Have I Got News For You'. For better or worse, watching one too many British comedy programmes has instilled in me a very British sense of humour — preferably understated and certainly never taking itself too seriously.

Not only has this made my life more fun than it might have otherwise been, I'm convinced that it's also helped me in the workplace because a bit of humour can be very useful if applied sparingly. Be it to loosen up a tense meeting, strengthen relationships or emphasise a point, humour is a versatile way of advancing your interests at work. As a bonus, people generally like a bit of fun, so if done well your popularity (and awareness levels) should also improve — and who doesn't like to be popular?

Of course, using humour doesn't come without risk because occasionally you'll judge it wrong and will inadvertently offend someone, particularly in our current climate. However, in my opinion the benefits of humour outweigh those risks and it's worth getting in early to hone your craft. That way, later in life you're a bit more certain that what you're about to say will actually be funny, not cringey or offensive (or deathly boring).

A BRIEF INTERLUDE ON HUMOUR

To convince you of this and get you started, here is a quick roundup of Matthias' Uses Of Humour In The Workplace, in rough order of risk, from which you're welcome to pick and choose:

- **Simple jokes, aka dad jokes** (e.g., "I used to be afraid of hurdles, but then I got over it.") I recommend having a list of maybe three to five simple jokes up your sleeve that you can deploy to ease tension or boredom, or just to get a meeting a bit more engaged from the start. Obviously, introduce the fact you're making a joke before you unleash it (otherwise there may be confusion) but as long as the jokes are inoffensive and pre-tested for impact, then there's not much that can go wrong. *Difficulty: 3/10; Risk: 2/10.*

- **Non work related anecdotes or content** (e.g., any funny current-affairs topic or you can always show people a photo of your cat making a face). Another simple way to break the ice, if you're looking for something a bit more engaging than the weather. Just make sure your story is actually funny before you use it. *Difficulty: 5/10; Risk: 3/10.*

- **Self-deprecation** (e.g., "Next time I might even attach the agenda to the email I sent.") It shows a great deal of self-confidence and because you're not taking yourself too seriously, it'll immediately put people at ease and might potentially catch them off guard — much harder to criticise you if you've already done it yourself! Having said that, it works best if you've been in the company for a while and have built up a good stock of credibility. *Difficulty: 6/10; Risk: 5/10.*

- **Work related anecdotes** (e.g., "I'm glad I managed to pass the exam on how to make the printer work...") If your example resonates, then it'll quickly establish a connection through a joint struggle. However, be careful what you choose as you may inadvertently offend some of the participants who don't see it as funny — or worse, end up the butt of your joke. *Difficulty: 6/10; Risk: 7/10.*

- **Mild ribbing** (e.g., "I see John is joining us on time today, and without his extra-hot toffee oat latte"). A great way to pass a potentially tricky message about someone's minor infringements such as tardiness or sloppy thinking. However, the other person is likely to be offended so you best be sure you're picking your battles carefully. *Difficulty: 5/10; Risk: 9/10.*

- **Sexual innuendos** (e.g., "That's what she said"). Can be really funny in private, but UNDER NO CIRCUMSTANCES GO THERE IN A WORK ENVIRONMENT. *Difficulty: 2/10; Risk: Off The Scale.*

I doubt that any of these were a surprise to you, but taken in the round it simply shows how many options you have to inject humour into the workplace to advance your objectives. But being funny isn't easy so be sure to practice early and often — in a controlled manner, of course.

Negotiating well (1): Why cinemas only sell giant tubs of popcorn

Pity poor cinema operators. 20 years ago, they were sitting pretty, with a monopoly on showing the best movies for the first six months of release, and even after that your only alternative was to buy or rent a DVD at extortionate rates to watch on your tiny analogue TV. Nowadays, your telly's twice the size, 1000x the resolution and with a decent sound system plus you have a near-unlimited choice of excellent fare streamed directly to your home. No wonder they're struggling to compete, with the smart ones trying to provide a more differentiated experience (reclining seats, hot meals) and all of them trying to make more money from ancillary sales. And who says cinema ancillaries, says popcorn — the association is almost Pavlovian: you think of cinema, you can practically taste the salty goodness.

For the cinema operator then, one key question is how to sell as much popcorn to each guest as humanly possible, which can be rephrased as: how do I ensure that each guest buys the insanely giant tub? This of course maximises profit given the low unit cost of the actual corn, and the fact that selling a small or a large tub takes roughly the same time. The answer is to *frame the customer's decision* so that the giant tub is significantly more attractive than the alternatives. Sure, you could price the different options at £3/£6/£9 to reflect their relative sizes — the giant one is three times the size of the small one, so it costs three times as much. However, this would give less greedy customers a genuine option to settle for a small tub and lose the cinema a potential £6 of revenue.

Instead, most cinemas will price the options at something like £7/£8/£9, which makes the small popcorn look stupidly expensive (intentionally so) but the giant one reasonably good value in comparison (which it is, except that most people didn't actually want so much popcorn in the first place).

If you look around, this tactic is everywhere, from Starbucks (the 'Venti' is twice the size of the 'Tall' for a nominal extra cost) to mobile phone contracts (100x the data for 2x the cost). However, the *framing of choices* doesn't always have to be aimed at getting people to pick the most expensive item: in software sales, for example, the objective is often to nudge customers towards the mid-priced option via a 'good, better, best' approach — sometimes rather unsubtly reinforced via a 'Recommended for you' or 'Most Popular' box around said option. Not only does this increase profits for the company, it also makes customers feel better because they have actively chosen the sensible option, thus proving to themselves they are neither a cheapskate nor overly profligate. A similar approach is used on restaurant wine lists — often featuring a 'cheap and nasty' wine so that customers trade up to the next level.

Here's the thing: what works for customer-facing decisions also works for internal decisions. So, when you're looking for approval for a particular project or expenditure, make sure of two things: Give the approver a choice and make sure you frame the options in such a way that your preferred one is the obvious answer. The reason this approach works is because it appeals to basic psychology[20]: Rather than asking someone to say yes or no to something (prompting a potential 'hang on a minute' gut reaction), you're asking them to pick their favourite choice — not only implying that approval is already assumed (it's not yes or no, it's yes to which one) but also actively appealing to their ego ("what do you think is best").

The most common way of framing choices is a version of the 'good, better, best' dynamic explained above, for instance if you work in engineering you could give three options of infrastructure resilience, if you work in marketing it could be three levels of ad campaign spend or if you work in customer service it could be three levels of response speed. However, there is also the option of creating the illusion of choice when it doesn't matter what option is chosen as long as the work is approved. Instead of asking your boss whether you should send a follow-up email to a sales contact, show two options and ask them which one they prefer. Instead of asking whether you're OK to run a promotion, make finance choose between two quite similar set-ups. The cynic in me thinks that coffee shops have also adopted this principle in offering Lattes and Cappuccinos: you think you're making a choice but the drink you get is often the same[21].

---

20 This is just a small window into the fascinating world of Behavioural Science. For a fun take on behavioural science in marketing, look up Nick Kolenda online.

21 I apologise to all the Italian readers I've offended here. Yes, I know those drinks are not the same, but many coffee shops do not.

For an even higher chance to get your way (say, on the most important projects) you should go further than presenting options and aim to 'hold the pen' on the entire conversation. By this I mean actually driving the process, including the timing, agenda and attendees of meetings and in particular the content of written documents. While increasingly these tend to be collaborative efforts using tools such as Google Docs and Microsoft SharePoint, presentations still require somebody to be in overall charge of the story, slides and timings. It can be a thankless task at times involving the herding of many cats (and the occasional system crash), but she who wrestles control of the pen can invariably sway the conversation in her favour more easily. So if you have the opportunity, don't be shy! Get stuck in and (preferably subtly) nudge the story in your direction.

ACTION

Find a project or activity that requires approval (say, by your boss or by finance). First, write down your desired outcome — say, a certain amount of money to be spent or people to be allocated. Then, develop a couple of alternatives that are either 1) clearly worse, so that your preference becomes the obvious choice or 2) broadly similar so that you'd be happy with any of them. I suggest trying out your options on a willing friend, family member or colleague: It's important that you pitch it right, so you get the outcome that you expect! Finally, decide when and how to communicate your options to the chosen decision-maker.

Negotiating well (2): Getting my teenagers out of bed

I have two wonderful kids who at the time of writing are 17 and 14 (although by the time you pick up a second hand copy of this book on eBay, they might be 37 and 34!) who, like all teenagers, love to stay up past midnight and get up at lunchtime whenever they don't have school. Which makes me almost wistful — oh, those were the days!

Normally this isn't an issue, but occasionally I do need them to get up a little earlier, as on a recent skiing trip. Of course, skiing is crazily expensive, plus the conditions get worse as the day progresses, so you really do want to get started at a reasonable time. Here's how the discussion unfolded:

> **Me:** "Kids, we're getting up at 7.30 tomorrow so we can be on the slopes by 8.30"
> **Kids:** "Whaaaaaaaaaaat no that's insane"
> [Tense wait ensues]
> **Kids:** "OK how about we get up at 8.30, that'll still get us there by 9.30"
> **Me:** "I guess that's OK"

You might think I lost this negotiation, but you'd be wrong — my plan was all along to be there by ten, so I was even happy to cut the kids a few minutes' slack after their alarm. I just

NEGOTIATING WELL (2): GETTING MY TEENAGERS OUT OF BED

used a pretty standard tactic centred around the principle of *anchoring*, i.e. setting initial expectations at a certain level. This allows the other party to claim a negotiation 'win' because they managed to get you to move away from your anchor — not knowing that you were quite happy to settle for a much lower (or higher) number in the first place. Here's how it works:

- **STEP 1:** Open your negotiation with a proposal far beyond what you'd like to achieve (but not so far beyond to lose all credibility[22])

- **STEP 2:** Wait for your opponent to counter-offer at a level that is still acceptable to you

- (Or for advanced players, repeat both steps another time to eke out a little extra yet still allow your opponent to claim a small 'win')

I'm sure I haven't taught you anything dramatically new here and you've used this tactic yourself, perhaps unconsciously, from an early age. "Can I have ten sweets please gran" — "Alright, five sweets will do…" However, despite its obviousness, the anchoring tactic still works well if used correctly. Let's say you think you need another three heads in your team to cover a new geography. An anchoring approach might be asking for five to ten heads, as long as you can find a (semi-credible) way to substantiate this, say based on external benchmarking. This'll put a stake in the ground that you're serious about

---

22 Let's address the elephant in the room: Donald Trump uses this tactic all the time; I'll let you judge whether he's doing it successfully

the additional headcount and at the same time set off alarm bells that HR will need to have difficult negotiations with you down the line. But if you've pitched it right then it's unlikely that you'll get zero heads — particularly as companies often tend to 'haircut' all requests equally so the higher you can anchor, the higher the end result.

Of course, the effectiveness of the anchoring approach — and the choice of initial anchor — will depend on the situation and in particular the relative strength of each negotiating party: the stronger your hand, the higher you can aim. Here are a few questions to help you gauge it right:

- What's your relative level of knowledge and information? In the example above, you'll be in a stronger position if you're an expert in the field but HR is not.

- How much appetite for risk do parties have? As always, understand the motivations of your opponent before you engage them.

- What are your respective BATNAs? No, not BATMAN but BATNA: Best Alternative To Negotiated Agreement — an unnecessarily fancy expression for 'your plan B'[23]. If you have a strong alternative lined up, then by all means push really hard, whereas if the person you're negotiating with is your only option, then be more careful. And because it's all about relative strengths, also try and figure out your opposite number's BATNA, for the same

---

23 For more information, see Further Reading

reason: if they don't really have a good alternative to working with you, your position will be stronger.

Like any other skill, negotiation must be learnt and honed over time, so that you know what works most effectively. As the opportunities for doing so in the workplace may be limited (and the cost of failure may be high), I suggest using less important everyday situations as a reasonable proxy. Thinking of switching broadband providers? See how hard you can push on the monthly price or one-off benefits. Not too fussed about keeping your Apple TV+ or National Geographic subscription? Ask for 50% off and see what you get. Had a really bad experience with an airline? Request lots of compensation and see if you get half the amount.

I don't know about you, but I actually enjoy most negotiations because they're like playing a little game where you try and tilt the board in your favour. So I'd encourage you to do the same, pushing as hard as you can (but not too hard) and having some fun along the way. With a little preparation, you might be surprised at the results, especially if you have little to lose. Just remember this: Unless it's an extreme situation, always be friendly and courteous even in difficult negotiations — nobody likes to be shouted at so you're unlikely to achieve a good outcome by raising your voice. Instead, rely on your cunningly devised plan to do the work for you.

ACTION

Select an upcoming negotiation with a relatively specific and measurable outcome — say an amount of resources dedicated (heads or money) or the price you'll need to pay for a service. Ideally this would be an example from work, but it doesn't have to be. Pick your goal, then write down the strengths and weaknesses of both parties and use those to determine your starting anchor. Then find a way to put it into practice.

Setting prices: Restaurant 97 in Surbiton

I love food, although not as much as my wife does, for whom a tasty meal is the magic cure to all ills. As a result, we cook a lot at home — I'll make you a *Sachertorte* if you ever visit — but also try to have dinner out at least once a month, preferably in a restaurant we haven't visited before. Having lived in the same area for some time, over the years we've made it to most locally renowned eateries, with the exception of one: Restaurant 97 in Surbiton. And that's because their reservations — they only do tasting menus — go on sale on the first day of each month and are usually sold out by lunchtime. And I can't quite be bothered to set myself a reminder to sign up in time.

Your first reaction to this story might be: Great, well done Restaurant 97 for being so popular! They must be delighted to have such high demand. (And: how hard is it really to set yourself a reminder?) From a pure business perspective that is the wrong conclusion to draw. Really you should be saying: Why is Restaurant 97 leaving so much money on the table (as it were) by under-pricing their tasting menu? Because who says "this product sold out really fast" is really saying "this product was priced too low".

Pricing is possibly my favourite subject of all, because it's such a badly understood topic yet crucial to increasing profitability — any £ you manage to add to your price (assuming no reduction in demand) goes straight to the bottom line, so even a few percent can make a big difference. As an example, a £5 increase on a £100 product is only 5%, but if your profit margin was 5% (so, £5 originally) then you've just doubled it! Even if you rarely get involved in setting prices, it's useful to know that this lever exists so that you can use it when you get the chance.

Here's a crash course in pricing: The number one rule, from a seller's perspective, is to always *price to market*. Don't set the price according to what you personally think your product is 'worth', or what it cost you to make, or what competitors might be charging (although all of these are useful inputs). Instead, set the price according to the value that you create for customers, as expressed by their willingness to pay. This is assuming that your objective is not to sell as much as possible, as quickly as possible, but rather to maximise profits. As counterintuitive as it might seem, this often means *not* selling to certain customers in order to sell to others at a higher price and ultimately make more money.

In an ideal environment, you'd sell to different customers at different prices according to what they're willing to pay — an example is airline tickets, where flexibility, time to departure and other factors are used to vary the price of an identical seat. To a lesser extent, companies can manufacture multiple versions of essentially the same product — take the iPhone as an example with its different sizes and memories. The top end version will retail for more than twice as much as the cheapest one, but doesn't cost anywhere near twice as much to make. But even where this is trickier, such as in our example of the tasting menu, prices should be set as close as possible to the point of profit maximisation.

Ah yes, I hear you say, but how do I know where that point is? Or more specifically, what if I set the price of my product too high and no one wants to buy it? Surely, it's better to set the price too low, maybe leaving some money on the table, but be sure that I sell out? That risk does exist, so you don't want to go too crazy too quickly. On the other hand, if you never cross the line, you don't actually know where the line is! And you'd be amazed how much room you often have to push your prices up without really affecting volume — it all depends on the elasticity of your demand. The Economist newspaper, for example, has moved its per-issue price from £3 to £8 over the past two years and seems to be doing very well out of it. Sure, doing so can often be very uncomfortable because your salespeople (or customers) might complain that your product is now very expensive. But ultimately, if your customers continue to pay then once you get over the initial concerns, you'll have a lot more money to show for it. (As an aside, it's generally better practice to raise prices little and often rather than not at all and then by a lot, as customers are more likely to really notice the latter strategy.)

This brings us back to that tasting menu — seabass with rhubarb and samphire, anyone? — at Restaurant 97. Perhaps they were right to be a little cautious initially and test the market. Perhaps other restaurants were pricing at similar levels. Perhaps they have an unusually low cost structure. But once they discovered their ability to sell out within a couple of hours of opening, they should have taken the opportunity and increased the price. Given their strong demand, I'd be willing to bet they'd still sell out at £10 more — not quite as quickly, but sell out all the same. Let's say they sell 200 menus a week, that's another £2,000 of profit, not bad for a small restaurant. Yes, some of the regular customers might have complained, but most would have paid up, and in any case new customers (like me) would have been happy to take their place.

As so often in life, things aren't quite as black and white as this chapter makes them out to be — sometimes, there is a valid reason for leaving a bit of money on the table. Glastonbury for example is charging significantly less than it could, because it wants to remain accessible to a wide range of fans. Being regularly 'sold out' can drive word of mouth and thus demand over a longer period of time. IPOs like to underprice so the share price increases on the first day of trading (although that one *is* often crazy as companies literally leave *millions* on the table). And regular customers may purchase more often if they don't feel they've been pushed to the limit each time. Nonetheless, I remain convinced that there is often significant headroom in pricing decisions, and I encourage you to respond to any items that quickly sell out with an indignant shout of: "it's too cheap!"

ACTION

If you have a job that requires price setting of any sort (say in sales or revenue), then the action is quite simple: find a product whose price you can increase! If not, then your action is to cook a tasty meal for a friend/partner/colleague of your choice. Because good food is a surefire way to happiness and great friendships are priceless.

Managing people and projects: Let it go, let it go!

I recently went to visit a friend whom I met through a shared passion of the sport of orienteering, which involves running through forests, parks and towns with a map and a compass in search of little orange flags. Over the last few years, he's built a thriving orienteering club in a town where none previously existed — an impressive feat that's taken up untold hours of his time in creating maps, setting up races, organising youth training sessions and generally getting the word out. However, he's run into a problem: he's getting a bit exhausted from the effort and while he's successfully roped in helpers for some aspects (managing the start or collecting flags back in), nobody else has yet organised a race without him. "It just won't work", he says. "The other guys simply aren't good enough, they'll end up making a mistake somewhere."

Thing is, he's almost certainly right. Without him, the quality of the event is likely to be a little lower, and the chance of a mistake a little higher. However, he's also trying to grow his club into something sustainable in the long term and not burn himself out in the process. What to do? This is a dilemma faced by all founders and indeed by anyone who has people or project management responsibilities: How to grow while maintaining the high standards that you've established? And I'm afraid there is only one answer: Let it go. Delegate. Trust team members to make their own decisions, and yes, occasionally their own mistakes. It's the only way for you to expand your span of influence and really take the next step to accelerate your career, because even if you work 24 hours a day, you won't get as much done as a team can achieve.

Having said that very clearly, let me add some nuance. Letting go of direct control can be a very stressful experience for anyone, especially if your team really isn't as good as it could be. I'm not advocating to blindly trust everyone and suddenly be completely hands-off. That would probably be a recipe for disaster and is unlikely to set your team up for success, which should be the aim. However, you do need to start by letting go of the assumption that if you don't personally control everything, the world will fall apart — and actually mean it, unlike a CEO who when interviewing me said "I'm not a micro-manager, but I have to be in all the detail because I'm the only one who understands it properly"!

Once you've made that first mental leap, we can start talking about how to make your management experience a success. The best starting point is the concept of *Situational Leadership*, developed by Hersey and Blanchard in 1969[24]. Its essence is that your management style (and level of delegation) needs to be tailored to the situation you're in, according to 1) how motivated the individual is and 2) how skilled they are in the task at hand. On the one extreme, someone who's able and keen can indeed be managed with little supervision: agree their goals and ways of working, and let

---

24 Look online for more details

them get on with it. On the other extreme, someone who's neither motivated nor competent will need a lot more oversight: you do need to agree detailed action lists and regularly check on progress (and if their performance doesn't improve, they're probably not right for your team). Most individuals will sit somewhere in the middle so require a compromise approach of some sort, which you should discuss with them quite openly (e.g., "I'll be a bit more involved in this project because I know you're new to it" or "I'll leave it to you, but check in with me on anything big"). Don't assume that every team member will be as driven as you are and remember that situational analysis is only half of the puzzle, the other half being the person's underlying drivers and motivations, as explained in Section Three.

That's all very well, you might say, but delegation just takes too long. By the time I've explained the work to my team member, I could have done it myself, so what's the point? While this is a common argument, I'll stop you there as it's nonsense. Fair enough, it may be true initially but very quickly, it'll reverse as the second, third and hundredth time around they'll know what to do. In fact, you need to think of team members in a much more expansive way: They're not just there to execute more of your orders faster so that you become some kind of giant octopus who's able to be in eight places at the same time. Believe it or not, most team members can actually think for themselves and might come up with entirely new ideas that you hadn't considered, or a better way of doing things. They might even teach you something! Thus I'd actively encourage you to surround yourself with people cleverer than you — you'll develop a lot faster and it's really fun (if sometimes exhausting).

None of this is easy. Team members will make mistakes, or there could be misunderstandings. You'll lose some control. You'll end up over- or under-delegating because you've misread the situation. You might even be upstaged by a team member with superior skills. Good management is hard and most companies don't prepare their new managers for the task at hand even remotely well enough (although if your company offers a course for managers, grab it). Delegation also relies on trust, which is hard to build and easy to lose.

However, to really progress in your career, delegating effectively is the first step on the road to becoming a good manager. Here are a few more top tips:

- Find a balance between being approachable and being professional. You don't want your team members to think you're a work-issued robot, but regularly going clubbing with them probably isn't advisable either.

- Spend enough time on praising a job well done before moving onto the next challenge, so it doesn't become one endless climb without ever appreciating the views.

- Accept that one's personal life should always trump one's office life. If your team member needs time to sort out an issue, show empathy and support them in doing so.

- Take time out to develop people and talk about the future, even if work is busy.

- Coach people to solve their own problem, rather than solving it for them. But don't overdo it — if a team member genuinely asks you to sort something out after they've exhausted all other options, then do it.

The next step on this journey is management of bigger teams and then eventually, true leadership through inspiration and vision. I could write an entire book just on those topics and if this first one becomes a success, then maybe I will!

ACTION

If you're a people manager, pick a team member who's ready for more delegated responsibility. Devise a plan on how to do this, including 1) what you'll delegate; 2) how you'll set them up for success and 3) how you'll balance control and freedom. If not, use a project in which you could delegate some of your work to someone else. Then follow the same instructions.

Reinventing things: Never waste a good crisis

In addition to orienteering, my second sport is running — more by necessity than by design, because to do well in orienteering you must both run fast and read a map well. So for better or worse I've run an average of three days a week for as long as I can remember. It's just what I do, except when I don't because occasionally I get injured (most often it's the calf) and then the routine gets turned upside down.

If you also do a sport at a reasonable level of competitiveness, then you'll know that not being able to do the thing that you always do can be really tough. Your friends are still going, you're likely to miss some competitions and you're just a bit lost as to how to use your newfound spare time. Initially, this might put you in a bit of a funk. You wander around the house slightly dejectedly. You're a bit crankier than usual. You feel very sorry for yourself.

Here's the deal: No one likes a grumpy bugger and it's not good for your health either. So when a crisis hits you, allow yourself a short time to self-indulge but then move into action mode: Use the crisis as an opportunity to reinvent the way you're doing things. However bad it might seem initially, I'm convinced that you can come out stronger on the other side.

With my focus on running (and my advancing age), I'd neglected my core for too long, having done barely any flexibility and strength work. So after many years of thinking about it, I reluctantly joined a gym. Ugh! Indoors, really not my thing, or so I thought. Turns out I actually love it, particularly the fancy weight machines and — weirdly enough — the steam room. I still can't run properly and while I miss it, I've built up a decent core in the meantime.

I'll grant you that I might be stretching the use of the terms 'crisis' and 'reinvention' with my running example — it's not exactly existential even if it sometimes felt that way. At the other extreme of the spectrum, think of Netflix who in the late 2000s faced bankruptcy from their dwindling DVD business only to reinvent themselves as a content-creating streamer. Or Airbnb doubling down on their core experience during Covid, only to re-emerge twice as strong. Or indeed think of those companies that didn't, like Kodak.

You never know quite what crises you might face in your career, but one thing is clear: it's unlikely to be a linear path. So I'd like to encourage you to stay positive and see the opportunities, not the problems, if any of the following happens to you:

- An injury or illness means that you're prevented from doing something you love. Try to think: What new hobby or passion can I try out?

- The part of the company that you work in is downsized or sidelined. Try to think: Can this be an opportunity to do something different?

- Your work life balance suddenly changes, perhaps because of a long distance commute.

Try to think: How can I use this time productively? How can I adapt my routine?

- A senior person (perhaps your manager) quits, and the future setup of your department is unclear. Try to think: How can I step into some of that vacuum?

- Your big project has failed or didn't reach its objectives. Try to think: What's next out there? How can I learn from the failure?

- You lose your job or don't get the promotion that you wanted. Try to think: How can I use this opportunity to pivot my career?

On that final point, I've twice been made redundant and once chose to leave a company with only a rough idea of what might come next. Those situations are never easy and of course it helps if there is no immediate financial pressure to find another role, because of a pay-off or a 'rainy-day fund'[25], but they're definitely opportunities to rethink your priorities and consider new options. While I only ended up making minor changes (from digital to industry, from full-time to interim roles), there are plenty of examples of full career pivots to entirely new roles, industries or locations.

And crises don't have to be as traumatic as injuries or job changes to be a catalyst for reinvention. If your usual marketing channels no longer produce a good return, can you

---

25 Also known as the 'fuck-off fund'. If you can afford it, I highly recommend you put away some money so you can have more flexibility to quit a job when it's not right, or not take the first offer that comes along. Six months' (conservative) outgoings is a good benchmark to aim for.

try new ones? If your traditional customer base is shrinking, can you find alternatives? If your budget is cut, can you bring work in-house?

I'm afraid that I can't promise all crises will turn into opportunities for you. As a Manchester United supporter, I've now been waiting for over ten years for that to come true and every time I feel it's getting better, it actually gets worse! But what I can promise is that a positive, 'growth' mindset and a relentless desire to learn and do better next time will help you reach your goal in the end, even if it doesn't happen immediately.

ACTION

If you're in a crisis situation at the moment (and I'll let you set the threshold for 'crisis'), take a deep breath, settle yourself and focus on the future: How can you turn this crisis into an opportunity? What does 'great' look like in three months' time?

If you're not, instead ponder a what-if scenario, specifically what if your company went bust tomorrow and you lost your job? Once you're past the initial shock (and ignoring any financial constraints for the moment), how could you leverage your experience into something even better going forward? What would you build on and what new things would you want to learn? You never know, it might happen one day and in any case it's great preparation for the final section of this book — how to get a better job.

REINVENTING THINGS: NEVER WASTE A GOOD CRISIS

PART 5

HOW TO GET A BETTER JOB

And so we come to the crux of this book. (Finally! I hear you shout.) Of course, doing a good job is in and of itself a laudable aim and I hope that you've taken some 'mini fist bumps' from putting one or the other of my recommendations into practice. I also hope that you've learnt a few things about yourself and maybe improved the odd relationship with a tricky coworker.

Ultimately though, you won't be moderately successful without a promotion or two along the way, either within your existing company or moving to a new one. These days, career paths have become pretty squiggly so it's no longer necessary to follow a predetermined path from say analyst to associate to manager — although consulting firms at least still operate in this way and most companies have job 'levels' of some sort. But to reach the goal you've set yourself at the beginning of this book, it's likely that you'll want to formally move up (or across) the ladder.

Doing well in your current role is of course a prerequisite for this — well most of the time anyway, sometimes you just get lucky — but it's rarely sufficient. You also need to look out for opportunities and then grab them with both hands when they appear. That's what this final section is about. First, we'll figure out together where you are now and where you might want to go next. Then, I'll give you some tips on how to get there — either through internal promotions or finding a new role externally.

We'll end on a few thoughts about how to succeed in a new role, but let's cross that bridge when we come to it. First, let's get you that better job.

Defining your 'value proposition'

Reflecting back on my career choices, I've often wondered what life would have been like if I'd discovered my vocation at an early age. What if, one day, I had an epiphany and woke up knowing that I wanted to be a baker. Or a dentist. Or a tax accountant specialised in offshore 'optimisation arrangements'. How much easier (though perhaps more boring) life might have been then, with only relatively limited choices to make and a well-trodden career path ahead.

It didn't work out that way and when I left university I didn't have a clue what I wanted to do, so I spent my first six years in strategy consulting — a way to keep options open which actually set me up well for the rest of my career. The industry may no longer have the best of reputations but it certainly taught me a lot of basic skills like data analysis, logical thinking and presenting arguments to senior clients, so if you have a chance to be a consultant for a while I'd still recommend it. Only in my early 30s did I start to specialise in the commercial aspects of a business: still not the result of a grand plan, but it was the function that seemed to suit me best.

Nowadays a non-linear career path is much more common than it used to be, and certainly in the absence of said epiphany, keeping your options open in your 20s is no bad thing. However, as you traverse your 30s I'd strongly recommend that you start narrowing down a little and developing some specialities in order to offer a more unique value proposition.

Corporate life is ultimately a pyramid with a lot of junior people and only a few senior ones, so if you want to stand out as you move up, you'll need to develop a clearer articulation of who you are and what you can bring. A crisp elevator pitch of "I'm the xxxxxx guy/gal" will come in handy as you move through an organisation's ranks or into a new company, and "I'm the clever generalist who can do a bit of everything" just isn't going to be as useful as "I'm your digital marketing expert", "I deliver complex engineering projects" or "I sell biotech solutions" come age 40. This is especially true for interacting with headhunters, as we'll see later.

ACTION

Imagine you are in an elevator with the CEO of a company that you admire and would love to work for. You have 15 seconds to introduce yourself and want to focus on the value you can add to that company. What do you say? And what would you ideally like to say (but might not quite be able to)? Write down your answer, which could be a mixture of functional, industry and skills expertise.

As you think about this action, you should remind yourself of a couple of answers you gave right at the beginning of the book. What does success mean to you? And how would you articulate your personal brand? The action should draw on both, but is subtly different in that it describes what you can offer a company now or in the near future. Eventually, that CEO will want to know about your longer-term aspirations and indeed what you're like as a person, but for now you need to keep it focused on your business value proposition.

While this chapter is a little too much about me for my taste, I thought I'd share my own answer to the action above. It's "I grow B2C businesses using customer insight and data, from strategy to execution, inspiring teams across multiple cultures", which — being honest here — isn't as differentiated as I'd like. As a commercial generalist, I can fit into a variety of roles and industries, but on the flipside, my experience is tricky to pinpoint especially if compared to others with a more directly relevant functional or industry profile. Not that I'm complaining, but job searches would definitely have been easier had I pursued a narrower profile earlier in my career (if only I'd known), which is why I'm recommending it to you. Hey, I never said I was perfect!

Developing your career: Get a mentor, or two

A little while ago I was chatting to a junior colleague over lunch. "I haven't had any career development chats in ages", he complained, "how will I ever get promoted"? His concern was far from unique: we're all so busy every day that finding time to step back and think about the future is really tricky.

But here's the thing about career development: it's not a *reactive* thing that's done to you, like an annual review or a drugs test (which can happen, I needed one to work for Eurostar)! To be truly effective, career development needs to be a *proactive* effort that you own and drive yourself. Of course, your organisation should support you in defining your career objectives and then in finding ways to address them, such as training courses or stretch assignments. But ultimately, if you don't drive your own career then it won't advance anywhere near as fast — so you need to take action.

We should start with a definition of career development. For me, it's the acquisition of new skills with the express intention of securing a bigger job in the near future. Which poses two key questions: What are those skills that you need to learn, and what is that bigger job? Though not necessarily in that order, as it's often the target job that will determine the skills that you need to pick up.

Hopefully, by now you'll have a rough answer to both of those questions. You do after all have your value proposition as a short-term guide as well as your definition of moderate success as a longer-term aim. You've also written down your personal brand in Section 1 and considered enough work scenarios in the other sections to know what you like and dislike, what your strengths and weaknesses are.

You might therefore be reasonably expecting the action from this chapter to be to write down your next target job and the skills required to get there, and indeed this is what I had originally planned (and you're still welcome to do it if you're clear enough). However, this really is one of those questions where outside help and advice can work wonders — so what you write down is less important to me than whose advice you seek.

Of course, the first thing you should do is book a career development session with your manager, if you haven't already done that. While you're in charge of your own career, your manager still has a duty (and hopefully an interest!) in helping you shape your goals and then enabling you to achieve them, usually by co-creating a personal development plan (or PDP). Typically, this will have up to five development objectives (such as, 'improve presentation skills' or 'learn the basics of financial accounting'), each with a timeline and some concrete next steps. But your manager may also have their own agenda and their first priority will be for you to deliver your business outcomes, before moving onto your wider career goals.

Therefore, I'd really like to encourage you to find someone else with whom to discuss your career, in the shape of a 'mentor', being a senior person you know who can give you career advice based on their life experience (as distinct from a 'coach' who typically focuses on specific skills in the short term, which can also be really useful should you need it). If nothing else, you'll add another voice to your extended support team. Here are some tips for choosing the right one:

- Aim high but not too high — find someone from whom you can really learn but who isn't so busy that they'll either decline or cancel meetings last minute

- Look both inside and outside of your current company[26]

- Flatter them by asking for their advice and counsel, making it hard to say no

- Suggest meeting for breakfast rather than lunch, because there's likely to be less competition for their time at 8.30am than at noon

- Be clear on your expectations from the outset: what are you trying to achieve?

Ultimately, whom you choose really depends on your personal circumstances, but to illustrate, over the years my mentors have been ex-bosses (a good choice if you got on well), senior managers in other departments and more recently a good friend who's at a similar career stage to mine. And of course, you don't have to stop at a single mentor — if you have the time and contacts, then by all means go for two!

---

[26] Either can work, but if you choose someone inside your company, pick someone from a different department so their thinking isn't too swayed by your day to day responsibilities.

Once you've secured the right person(s), I'd typically recommend meeting every couple of months or so to keep a good rhythm going but give enough time in between meetings to action some of the discussion points. At each meeting, make sure you come prepared with ideas and questions — don't just sit there expecting the mentor to give you the answer (which, if they're a good mentor, they won't do anyway). And don't expect a mentor relationship to last forever — some do, but some reach a natural conclusion after six months or a year.

To be clear, having a mentor isn't the immediate solution to your career concerns. For a start, it will take some time to secure one and then set up that first meeting. And the meeting won't in itself change anything: You'll still need to take action thereafter to get that stretch assignment or training course within your organisation, or indeed to effect a change to a new company (more on that later). However, the right mentor can transform the outlook on your career so it's well worth investing the time.

ACTION

Identify and approach a suitable mentor, then book in a time and place for the first meeting to give it the best chance of actually happening.

Getting promoted (1): Know the process(es)

Do you think your company's performance evaluation and promotion processes are tricky to understand, deliver unfair outcomes or are rigged against you? If so, you're not alone: trust in HR processes is generally relatively low despite the HR team's best efforts to the contrary. And that's because in practice, most evaluations and promotions retain a significant element of subjectivity — a bit like Premier League football, but without the VAR — leaving them open to debate and questioning. But rather than complain (which is unlikely to help and certainly isn't going to endear you to HR or management), you should focus your energy on understanding the 'rules of the game' and then use them to your advantage. Here's how.

PERFORMANCE EVALUATION PROCESS

Before we look at promotions, let's start with performance evaluations — after all, if your performance score isn't high enough, you're unlikely to be considered for promotion in the first place. Most companies run an annual performance review process, sometimes supplemented by quarterly or half-yearly checkpoints. The end result is normally a score for each employee, often using a variation of this 5-point scale:

5: Exceptional performance
4: Above-average performance
3: Expected performance
2: Below-average performance
1: Terrible performance

Some companies will invert the scale (with 1 being the best), and some might avoid numbers altogether and opt for words such as 'Outstanding', 'Great', 'Good', 'Needs Improvement' or similar, but the principle remains the same. In some instances, demonstrating company values is assessed separately (the 'how' vs the 'what') or incorporated into the overall score. And in others, employees will be given an additional rating of 'potential', reflecting not how they're performing today but what potential they have to move up in future.

The key question, however, is not how the scale is defined but how ratings are determined — what are the criteria and who is involved in the decision-making? This is what you need to find out and then use to your advantage as much as possible. In theory, it should be easy. Your individual goals are set at the start of the review period and at the end you have an honest discussion with your manager to agree your score. In practice however, it's rarely that simple, because there is always subjectivity involved and often your manager will not decide on their own.

Your first objective, of course, is still to convince your manager that you're (significantly) above average and doing great work throughout the year will put you in the best possible starting position. However, you also need to manage the process in your favour by (1) setting achievable targets in the first place; (2) regularly checking that you're on track;

(3) gathering supporting evidence and (4) preparing the end of year conversation really well.

Unfortunately, getting your manager onside isn't usually enough, because after individual assessments normally comes the departmental (or company) calibration process, and that's where the real fun starts. Managers have a tendency to inflate scores, because it makes for easier conversations with their team and because they genuinely believe that their team is the best in the company. But not everyone can be above average, so begins a protracted haggling phase: usually a combination of peer reviews ("I can't believe you've given Arnold a 4, he's never done anything useful for *me*...") and top-down pressure by HR ("We can't have more than two 4s in your team, you decide who they are").

So your second, almost more important objective is to ensure your high score survives the calibration process! For this you need to make sure that (1) you've equipped your manager with all the right arguments and examples to fight your corner and (2) the other people around the calibration table know who you are and have seen your great work. Perhaps you can proactively talk to them, or copy them into an email? Whatever you do, don't leave it up to chance.

ACTION 1

Understand how the evaluation process at your company actually works, end to end — both the formal (written down) part and any informal parts. Be clear on the evaluation criteria, the timelines and the decision makers (including any calibration). Then draw up a strategy to maximise your chances of a high rating at the end of the year.

PROMOTIONS PROCESS

If this chapter feels quite heavy already, I'm afraid it doesn't stop here — securing a good performance rating is necessary, but not sufficient, to secure your promotion. So let's move onto part two.

Normally, promotions work in a very similar way to evaluations, but with a higher level of scrutiny given their importance. Instead of performance ratings, organisations typically have 5-10 codified job levels, but these are not typically standardised across companies, as these examples from my past experience show:

- Analyst, Associate, Project Leader, Manager, Associate Partner, Partner — BCG 2004[27]

- Level 21 (entry level) to Level 28 (director) — eBay 2008, don't ask me why

- Band A (entry level) to Band F (manager), plus senior managers after that — Eurostar 2014

- Level 7 (entry level) to Level 0 (C-suite) — Trainline 2024

- Level 7 (entry level referee) to Level 1 (Premier League) — FA 2024[28]

Your approach to securing a promotion should therefore be quite similar to that of securing a high performance rating. Of course, do great work so you put yourself in the best possible

---

27 Consulting levels are reasonably, but not completely, standardised
28 I'm also a qualified football referee, and Level 7 sounds quite impressive even if it's not

position (and step up where possible, as described in the next chapter.) But in parallel, make sure you understand and use the process to make it happen, by answering these questions:

1. What is the level structure in *your* company and where are you currently placed?

2. What additional skills are required at next higher level up? In larger organisations, this should be formally documented in a 'skills matrix' with headings such as 'analytics', 'strategy', 'innovation', 'teamwork' etc. — at eBay this was called the Level Contribution Framework. In smaller companies, you may have to check with HR

3. Where are your main gaps and how can you address them? You should discuss this together with your manager, but your mentor should also help you here

4. How and when are decisions made? Often this is only once or twice a year unless circumstances are exceptional

5. Who are the decision makers (including any calibration process)? Do they know who you are and what you do?

6. And whether a more senior role needs to be officially available, or whether you can get promoted 'in role'? While the latter is a good start because it'll mean more money and a fancier title, eventually you'll want a whole new role with a larger span of responsibility

ACTION 2

Use the questions above to draw up a strategy that maximises your chances of landing a promotion, adding a target date and key next steps.

You might not believe me, but in most companies the HR team is trying really hard to create a fair and clearly documented process for performance evaluations and promotions. Rather than complain about any inherent bias, you need to use these processes to your advantage, leaving the company little option but to reward you.

Getting promoted (2): Step up!

Even if the previous chapter might have suggested it, getting promoted isn't *all* about process. While understanding and following the rules (and occasionally, gaming them to your advantage) is a key part of the puzzle, it also helps if the promotion just *feels right* to key decision makers, because it'll make it easier to approve and easier to defend to anyone who's asking why. So please don't come away with the idea that ticking the right boxes is all it takes — even if that were true, you'd likely be quite ill-prepared for your new role, causing problems down the line.

To illustrate, let me share with you possibly the single most profound piece of career advice I've ever received... drumroll please...: *If you want to be a Director, act like one!* Did you expect something deeper? Let me add some context: I had been at Eurostar (the train operator) for many years in various Head Of roles, and was becoming increasingly frustrated that I wasn't being promoted to Director, even though I seemed to be doing a good job and hitting my targets. (Never mind that no Director level opportunities were available and back then companies didn't just invent them to keep employees happy. That's happening more nowadays.)

My mistake was to channel my frustration into perceived blockers, rather than opportunities. So I might have said things like, "if only I were a Director, I could have made this decision" or "I'm really looking forward to being promoted so I can spend more time on strategy", reinforcing the fact that indeed I wasn't yet at that level[29]. Instead, I should have channelled my anger into some positive energy to prove that I could operate at that higher level already — *if you want to be a Director, act like one!*

The idea here is to channel your inner Elle Woods. (You haven't watched 'Legally Blonde'? Fix it.) After being admitted to Harvard Law School against the odds, Elle takes over a big court case while still only a summer intern by stepping up with confidence and acting the part, despite her limited experience. I'm not proposing you go quite that far and pretend to be the CEO when you're currently an analyst, but it's definitely true that pre-emptively stepping up to a higher level, at least occasionally, increases your chance first of promotion and then of success in the new role. If you're seen to operate at a higher level (and successfully as well), then the promotion decision becomes easy: in an ideal world, you want decision makers to say "oh, I thought she already was a Director" when your name comes up.

Clearly this is easier said than done, but it's not as hard as you think — it all starts with a mindset shift, which is entirely within your control. Don't be frustrated at your lower-than-desired level, be excited about what comes next and approach each day as if you were already operating a step up. *If you want to be a Director, act like one!* Of course you have to first decide what that actually means, for which you should

---

[29] I don't think I actually said those things but they'll do for illustrative purposes.

take inspiration from the HR documents described in the previous chapter as well as your colleagues who are already in those roles. Typically, it involves taking more responsibility for setting goals and making decisions and checking in with your manager less often: Asking for forgiveness if something goes wrong rather than asking for permission to do it in the first place.

Depending on your situation, you could try and do this together with your manager — transparently telling them you'd like more responsibility and asking them for help in getting there. Or, you could just get on with it and see what happens: A higher-risk but potentially faster method. I'm not talking about changing everything that you do overnight, but finding those opportunities (in group projects, for example) where you can step into a gap; or trying out a new approach in your day to day processes. An ideal scenario here is if a temporary step-up role appears (say a parental cover or leadership of a project), which I'd encourage you to grab with both hands.

Getting promoted isn't easy, because a few stars need to align for you to get the nod — your performance, an available opportunity, the decision makers, the company funds. So don't lose faith if it doesn't happen as quickly as you expected, but you can maximise your chances of success by knowing the rules and in the meantime just stepping up regardless. *If you want to be a Director, act like one!*

ACTION

First, pick a colleague whom you admire, who is operating at the (higher) level to which you are seeking promotion, and write down their name. Second, consider your current ways of operating: How you decide what to do, how you interact with others, how you seek approval. Then ask yourself: If that colleague was in your shoes, how would they behave differently? Write down a couple of the key differences and then put them into practice. Don't be too conservative!

A Brief Interlude on luck

Have you heard the joke about the investment banking recruiter throwing away half of job applications without looking at them? When a colleague asked them to explain, their answer was: "Well, we wouldn't want to hire anyone who is unlucky now, would we?"

I don't believe in luck. I believe in making your own luck[30] and this is one of the central tenets of this book — be proactive and take the opportunities that present themselves. Start from the assumption that something is possible or allowed until told otherwise, not the other way around. Don't wait for others to decide things for you.

But so often, people miss chances because they're afraid to try. "There can't be any tables available at this restaurant today, look at how popular it is", they'll say. But did they ask, with a smile and perhaps an indication that they'll spend some money on the wine? "Our supplier will never agree to a change in contract terms", they'll say. But have they actually tried offering something else in return? "I'll never get this job", they'll complain. But have they applied and written an impassioned cover letter?

---

30 I realise that this is much easier for me to say, coming from a relatively privileged background, but the principle applies to everyone.

Don't sit there and complain about how unfair things are — it might well be true, but complaining is unlikely to improve the situation, so get up and sort it out. It's all your fault, remember?

And yet.

Like it or not, there *is* an element of luck in your career path. Sometimes, there just isn't a role to get promoted into, however amazing you might be. Conversely, your manager might quit just at the right time and you're the only sensible candidate available, so up you step without so much as an interview. Your company might be hit by an external shock and go bust, or it might hit a lucky break and become enormous overnight. You might find out about a great new role with a perfect fit, but perhaps it's just been filled last week. ("Isn't it ironic", Alanis would say.)

The best way of reconciling this somewhat contradictory logic is to think of your *long-term* career path as a nice smooth arc going up and to the right. This is the luck you're making for yourself by going for opportunities and believing in yourself. Underneath that trend line however, the *day-to-day* experience is more unstable, with some swings up and down. That's the luck you can't control, which sometimes goes in your favour and sometimes doesn't.

So, refuse to believe that luck is a thing until you have to accept that luck is a thing. That way, you'll be the luckiest person alive.

Fantastic jobs and where to find them

While I truly hope that you'll be able to progress in your current company — learning skills, adding responsibility, getting promoted — sooner or later will come the point where you'll want to go somewhere different. Perhaps you get a call from a recruiter or a friend with a great opportunity, perhaps you feel stuck in your current role with no obvious path to progression, or perhaps you just fancy a change of scenery. Either way, switching companies is a big decision so I want to make sure you get it right. (Of course it's not irreversible and nowadays spending a few shorter stints with multiple companies is perfectly acceptable, but it's still better if there's a good fit in the first place.) So — let's define the right job for you, before focusing on how you might actually find it.

WHAT'S THE RIGHT JOB FOR YOU?

Think back to the last time you moved house. I bet it wasn't an easy call. Between the location, the transport links, the cost, the neighbours, the size, the recreational opportunities, there are so many variables that you're unlikely to ever find the truly perfect place and worse, you need to make a decision on a property today without knowing whether a better one will come along tomorrow. It can be fairly gut-wrenching.

Choosing a new job is very similar. Between the title, the location, the pay, the manager, the culture, the benefits and the potential for promotion, there's a myriad of information to consider — and you equally don't know if something better will come along soon after. Of course, as with housing you might just find *the one*, in which case I'm delighted. But it's unlikely, so to point you in the right direction I recommend a fairly simple job inventory. Let's do that now, even if you're happy where you are.

ACTION 1A

First, create two columns on a page entitled: 'Things I like about my job' and 'Things I don't'. Then fill each column with at least ten (yes, ten!) items. This could literally be anything no matter how big or small, from 'growing sales' or 'my colleagues' or 'the pay' all the way to 'the free breakfasts' or 'the view from my desk'. Just go with the flow and write down what naturally comes to mind — be honest though, there's no point pretending.

FANTASTIC JOBS AND WHERE TO FIND THEM

ACTION 1B

Second, on a new page write the header 'What's important to me in a new job'. Use the inventories you made in Step 1 to pick out the 5-10 truly key things that you'd want from your new job — keeping some of the aspects you like and addressing some that you don't. Going forward, assess any new job opportunities against this list! If you're really keen, you could even give the criteria different weights to reflect their relative importance.

I want to add a reality check here. You might think that switching companies is a great way to get that bigger, better paying job that you can't quite reach where you are today. Unfortunately, nine times out of ten that isn't going to happen, especially at more senior levels. In my experience, it's much easier to move up *inside* your current company than *across* into a new company, and for obvious reasons. Your existing employer already knows and trusts you, so is more likely to give you the benefit of the doubt, whereas a new employer doesn't and learning a new company *and* a bigger role at the same time is a tough ask.

This doesn't mean you shouldn't try and aim higher, and certainly earlier on in your career there is scope to move across *and* up at the same time, at least a little bit. But I'd encourage you to evaluate any new company not just on the role they're offering you now, but on the potential to move up over the next few years.

HOW WILL YOU FIND A NEW JOB?

Now that you're equipped with a good checklist, you need to find some roles to evaluate! This is a lot harder than it sounds, because the job market remains incredibly fragmented and opaque, despite all the recent advances in other areas of HR technology. Perhaps AI will finally fix this issue, but for now you need to work extra hard to make sure you're aware of all the relevant jobs going, or more importantly, that the jobs are aware of you. Here's how to improve your chances:

Networking

It's not going to come as a surprise that networks are a really powerful way of finding new roles, because the first thought of a hiring manager will be: "Do I know anyone suitable for this role already?" Which could be you, or it could be someone who knows you, so the bigger (and more active) your network, the better your chances. Be proactive first in meeting new people (at work, at industry events, through friends, etc.) and then make sure you keep in touch, preferably via LinkedIn, which certainly in the UK remains the best platform.

I realise that networking takes time and I'm not suggesting that you go crazy and do nothing else for a while. However, connections soon add up so my strong recommendation is to start early in building your network, then invest the time to grow and develop it. Think of it as a little oak sapling that over the next 20 years will turn into a mighty tree.

Headhunters

The principle about networking extends just as much, if not more, to headhunters. Whenever you have a chance to speak to a headhunter, say yes even if the role might not be immediately relevant — you'll be added to their books, which increases your chance of being contacted when a more suitable job comes up later. But don't expect headhunters to proactively look for a role for you — they have a lot more candidates interested than roles to fill, so you need them more than they need you. In the next chapter, we'll look at the dynamics this imbalance creates.

Your LinkedIn profile

This is your shop window, so take a tutorial to exploit its full potential — from photo to headline to background image to keywords and more. And make sure that the content reflects the image you want to portray, particularly with the next job you'd like to have in mind. For extra impact, consider occasionally posting on LinkedIn, but it's not easy to get cut-through: You'll really need to have something thought provoking to say, as merely showing off your latest achievement is unlikely to resonate.

Job ads

To be honest with you, I'm pretty cynical about applying for jobs on job boards (such as Reed) or via LinkedIn. That's because I must have applied for hundreds of them without any success, and in most cases without so much as a reply, perhaps unsurprising given that enormous number of applications for the average job. However, it may also be me: I do know of people who've found jobs on LinkedIn, so it's at least worth keeping an eye on. Just don't get your hopes up too much.

Contacting companies directly

This can be a surprisingly fruitful avenue if you have target companies in mind. You have two options here — the obvious one, which is to keep an eye on company recruitment pages, sign up to their 'new job alerts' and be one of the first applicants. Or the less obvious one, to write a direct email to one of the senior executives with your pitch. If that sounds a bit hopeless, I've written six emails to company CEOs in my time and received five replies — not a bad hit rate, right? This approach however only works if your email is personal, targeted and to the point. Do your research to address specific issues or reference particular events, then make your killer pitch, and you never know where it might lead.

Finding a new job is all about being in the right place at the right time, and knowing what you want. While you can't normally force the situation (very few companies will create a job for you if they don't have a vacancy, no matter how brilliant you are), you can certainly improve your chances of success by being proactive. So get started today.

ACTION 2

From the options above, pick the one that resonates most and make an action plan to either (1) expand your network, (2) contact relevant headhunters, (3) check out job boards (4) update your LinkedIn profile or (5) identify three target companies and someone to contact there. If you can't decide, I'd recommend the final option because it'll force you to have a think about which companies would be top of your list.

Working with headhunters: It's not you, it's them

The first time a headhunter calls you is quite a cool experience. "Hello, I'm from Look & Find, the international search firm. I wondered if you'd be interested in a job opportunity that I'm working on..." Once you've established this is not in fact a prank call, it can give you quite a buzz. Someone is interested in me for a new role! And they've proactively got in touch!

I still enjoy being called by headhunters, but nowadays it's accompanied by a healthy dose of realism. Because to work well with them, you need to understand that their business model is generally that of an advisor paid by clients seeking to fill a role. Therefore, the client's needs come first and it's the client that drives the timeline[31]. So don't be offended if a headhunter reschedules a call with you at short notice to speak to a client instead, or doesn't get back to you for an extended time while the client considers their options.

In addition, while there are only a limited number of clients, for most roles there are an almost unlimited number of reasonably qualified candidates. For you this has a few implications. Firstly, unless you have truly unique skills, don't kid yourself that headhunters would be really missing out if they

---

31 Of course, one day you might be the client!

didn't consider you. Yes, you're great, but so are many others, so stay humble and don't overplay your hand. Secondly, headhunters often go for the 'safe' options when compiling their shortlists. Yes, I'm sure you'd do well in a very different role, but there's often no need to take the risk. (Hence the need for a clear value proposition, as described earlier.) And finally, headhunters are unlikely to deeply care about you as a person (sorry headhunters, it's true!) because if needed, they can find a replacement easily enough.

It also means that headhunters will allocate exactly as much time to you as is required at every point in the process. This isn't to say that all interactions will be brief, but the typical timeline goes like this:

- Initial call to gauge interest and fit: perhaps 10-15 minutes (and don't expect much small talk)

- If there is interest and fit: a more in-depth screening call for up to an hour

- If you're through to the next stages: short briefing and update calls as required, driven entirely by the client's timeline

- If you're made an offer: as much time as you'd like! For once you have the upper hand

- If at any point in the process you're rejected by the client: Two minutes to communicate the decision, then zero. You are dead to them, at least until the next client calls.

All this makes for a very transactional relationship, which can come as a bit of a surprise to candidates initially. You basically operate on their terms given your limited leverage, and on the premise of *don't call us, we'll call you*.

This isn't to say that headhunters will never get you a job, in fact the very opposite: they've been responsible for placing me at least three times, for which I'm very grateful. You just need to adjust your expectations so you're not caught off guard. Here are a few useful tips to get the most out of the relationship:

- Accept that you're playing to their rules and their timelines

- Be easy to work with; make yourself available; don't play hard to get

- Don't expect the headhunter to have read your CV in much detail. If asked to "run me through your CV" (while they catch up), don't go through every detail but focus on your results, your impact and what you've learned. Keep it brief and ask whether they'd like to hear more

- Be open-minded about a role if a headhunter suggests it, but don't expect them to find you a role if there isn't one. Say you look forward to hearing back from them in due course

- Be positive at all times and sound excited about a role, even if you have major misgivings. Make yourself be loved first; there'll be plenty of time to raise concerns later in the process

- Ask for honest feedback as you progress, so you can proactively address any concerns
- Don't use the occasional lack of common courtesy on their part (not replying to emails, turning up late to meetings) as an excuse to do the same — always be fully prepared and professional
- Always stay polite, even if you feel like shouting! Understand that headhunters are highly capable but usually under severe time pressure. See life from their perspective

As an aside, while there are some bigger firms[32], the market is very fragmented, including an ever-changing set of 'boutique' headhunters and (given the big money on offer) a lot of micro-businesses run by one or two experienced recruiters. This makes it impossible to be aware of every firm (and every job) going, which is why it's particularly key to get yourself as widely known as possible and to pick up the phone when headhunters call.

As you become more senior, headhunters are an integral part of the recruitment process and you should rejoice when one of them gets in touch. You just need to know what to expect.

---

32 For senior roles, these are called the SHREK: Spencer Stuart, Heidrick & Struggles, Russell Reynolds, Egon Zehnder and Korn Ferry.

ACTION

First, polish your CV. Does the value proposition you've defined earlier in this section jump off the page? Is your CV clear and concise? Is it even up to date? Second, even if you're not actively looking, ask three friends or colleagues (in a similar field to yours) if they know any headhunters and would be happy to introduce you. Follow up with a personalised email introducing your value proposition and your CV, 'in case relevant opportunities come up in future'.

A Brief Interlude on job titles[33]

Once upon a time, in a land not far away, most UK companies had a relatively straightforward set of job titles. They'd typically be led by a *Managing Director* who had reporting to them a handful of other directors, including at least an *Operations Director* and a *Finance Director*. To them in turn reported heads of department, each with a number of managers.

Then one day, the *Managing Director* woke up and looked across the Atlantic where all their friends were called *Chief Executive Officer (CEO)*, which sounded much grander, so they decreed that henceforth, they too would adopt this title. This made the other directors very envious and they exclaimed: "We want to be Chiefs too"! After a few months of nagging, the CEO relented and kindly agreed that the *Finance Director* be elevated to *Chief Financial Officer*, starting a slow but inexorable domino effect. *Chief Operating Officers* were next and finally the floodgates opened to ennoble CPOs (confusingly, this can refer to Product or People), CMOs, CCOs, CROs, CTOs and many more which are still being invented.

All was quiet for a short period, but now that all the Directors had become Chiefs, it was the turn of the Heads to

---

33 Don't let anyone tell you that job titles don't matter. They're good for the ego - or bad if you're feeling short-changed - and are part of your external branding, so treat them as such.

become restless and ask to take over the vacated Director slots. The Chiefs could not resist the onslaught and acquiesced, and then on it went down the chain of command, so that everybody had a nicer sounding title than before while still doing the same work.

Our story however does not end here, as another American import has recently been spotted with increasing frequency: the *VP (vice president)*, a hitherto niche title limited to financial institutions. Unhelpfully, some VPs are quite senior (think extended executive team) whereas others are relatively junior, reporting to a *Senior VP* who in turn reports to an *Executive VP*. Deep in the woods you may also encounter the occasional *President*, who may or may not have any power and the now more ubiquitous *Chief of Staff*, who rarely has any staff but is nevertheless very influential in their role of senior sidekick to the CEO.

All this is leading to much confusion in the land. Is a *VP* above or below *Director*? Does a *Manager* actually manage anyone? How senior is *Senior*? And is there really a *C3PO* on the leadership team[34]? So beware, dear reader, that juicy job title may not be what meets the eye. Or perhaps it is, just make sure you find out during the recruitment process where it sits in the company hierarchy. Then negotiate hard and don't let yourself be fobbed off too easily. I can't promise you'll live happily ever after, but *Director* does have a nice ring to it, doesn't it?

---

34 This is a Star Wars joke. I apologise.

Impressing people at interviews: My top ten tips

I love interviewing, both on the giving and receiving end, as it were. Even if I end up being unsuccessful or not hiring the candidate in front of me, at least I'll have had an interesting conversation and learnt something — about the business, about myself, or occasionally about some other random trivia.

However, I realise that I might be in a minority and that interviews often terrify people, leading to sweaty palms (or worse: sweaty armpits), halting responses or complete brain freezes. Those reactions are perfectly normal, especially earlier on in your career (with less experience to fall back on) and of course, especially if it's a job you really, really want.

With that in mind, here are a my top ten tips for interviewing well. Short of convincing you that interviewing is fun, I'll get you to a place where you feel confident and ready to go — which is half the battle won.

1. **Understand your interviewer**
   Start with the bedrock of any successful meeting: understanding your counterpart, in this case the interviewer. Use their job title, the company culture and any other information you can find to adapt your approach and answers, following the principles of Section Three. If they're a creative person, give them stories; if they're

analytical, give them numbers. If the culture is collaborative, talk about people; if it's goal-oriented; talk about achievements.

Bonus: Figure out your interviewer's personal passion from their LinkedIn profile or other online sources and weave it into the conversation.

2. **Do your homework**
   There's really no excuse for not doing a minimum of research about the company offering you a job. Review their website, find some latest news or read their annual report, then have a few soundbites ready.
   Bonus: Actually use the company's product or service as a consumer. Go visit their shop, sign up to their mailing list, buy a product online, call their customer service line — lots of brownie points are available here as it's surprisingly rare.

3. **Be extra nice to assistants**
   As part of the process you'll likely come across EAs who'll schedule your meetings, junior HR team members who might take references and receptionists who'll show you to meeting rooms. Make an effort to be super polite and thankful to all of them — not only will it make them happy, it'll reflect positively on you as a candidate (and will make it easier to get favours later on, should you need them).

4. **Be clear on the why**
   You'll get asked lots of questions during an interview, but the two to which you need to have the clearest answers are these:

- "Why are you the best person for this job?" Make sure to have your crisp value proposition from earlier in the section ready. What makes you stand out?

- "Why is this job right for you?" Don't just give a boring answer about working for a great company or wanting a promotion. Show your enthusiasm and find something compelling, like 'to reach my mid-term career goal' or 'because the company values particularly resonated'.

5. **Tell good stories**
   Of course, you'll be asked many other questions, so make sure you've got well-rehearsed answers for the most common ones — typically touching on your key achievements, your ways of working, how you deal with challenges and (everyone's favourite) your weaknesses. You can find plenty of sample lists online! Practice your answers in advance and find the three key stories that resonate the most. These can typically be moulded to answer different types of questions (this is called 'bridging' in formal interviews) and should be really engaging to set you apart from the competition. As an example, I often use the launch of the London-Amsterdam route for Eurostar because it touches on strategy, execution and people but also highlights my multicultural experience.

6. **Embellish, but don't lie**
   Let's be (not fully) honest: Everyone takes a little bit of liberty with their CV when it comes to interviews. Was it

really you alone who came up with this great idea? Are those numbers truly like-for-like? So play the game, but don't be stupid and make up an outright lie, as you'll be found out eventually.

7. **Let them speak**
You might think that the objective of an interview is for you to share as much information as possible in the time available. You would be wrong. It's a two-way conversation to establish whether your interviewer can imagine working with you, which is a subtle difference. In fact, many interviewers are surprisingly keen to talk rather than listen, so give them that opportunity. Keep initial answers brief, then check whether they'd like you to expand further. This also allows you to take a deep breath occasionally, rather than just rambling on forever.
Bonus: If the meeting starts with "please talk me through your CV", give a high level overview and then check what further details are required. Under no circumstances spend 20 minutes running through every detail.

8. **Be easy to love**
Yes, you may have a lot of questions or concerns about the job for which you're interviewing. Is the commute worth it? What are the hours like? How fast is the company growing? In the early rounds of interviews, put them to one side because your objective is to make the interviewer fall in love with you. And that isn't going to happen if you come across as concerned or standoffish. By all means, ask those tricky questions and find a way to get

an outside view before accepting any offer, but early on be all smiles and flatter away.

Bonus: Asking a question about the company culture is a great way to identify any red flags while still sounding excited and engaged.

9. **Prepare good questions**

    Another really basic, but oft-forgotten aspect of interviews: In 90% of cases, interviewers will end the meeting by giving you the chance to ask questions. Make sure you have three to five zingers lined up in advance that showcase you as inquisitive and interesting rather than overly detailed and petty. Focus on strategy, objectives, team and culture. Or just try an old favourite: "What does success look like in this role?"

    Bonus: Don't ask about the next step in the process. You'll find out soon enough and it's just dull.

10. **Do reflect, but don't beat yourself up**

    Nobody will get every single question right or remember to make every single key point in an interview. So don't beat yourself up and remember that others aren't perfect either. Do however reflect on your performance and take learnings to do better next time.

    Bonus: If during the interview you realise you've missed something, don't hesitate to say: "I wanted to come back to that question you asked me earlier." It'll allow you to correct your mistake and as a bonus shows a good level of self-awareness and poise.

Ultimately, the success of an interview can often hinge on how self-confident you're feeling going into it. I'm not advocating coming across all cocky and arrogant (nothing will annoy an interviewer faster), but if you believe in yourself, take strength from your achievements, and prepare well, then good things will happen. It's fine to be 'nervouscited' but channel it into positive energy and enthusiasm rather than self-doubt. That way, you'll enjoy the process even if you don't get the job — and give yourself a higher chance that you will.

ACTION

Think back to a recent interview that didn't go as well as you expected. Use the checklist above to identify a few things you could have done better, and write these down for next time.

Succeeding in a new role: How hard can it be?

Congratulations! You've finally got the new role that you really wanted. While you might not quite have reached your definition of moderate success, you're certainly on the right path. You've got all the right experience and the interview process went really well. The people seem lovely too. What could possibly go wrong?

When I started a job as an Associate Consultant at BCG in Paris back in 2002, having just spent three years in consulting in London, I thought: How hard can it be? It's just the same thing again but in French. Turns out, very hard. Partly because my French was decent but not at business level but also because BCG had a very different culture from my previous employer: more serious, less fun and with higher expectations.

When I started a job as Revenue Director at Hand Picked Hotels back in 2016, having just spent seven years doing much the same at Eurostar, I thought: How hard can it be? It's just the same thing again but in hotels. Turns out, very hard. Partly because the financial dynamics were fundamentally different (1000 customers a day not 50 000) but also because Hand Picked had a very different culture — more operational, less automated, more consensus-driven.

While it happens more frequently than before, starting a new role is still a major milestone in most people's careers, and one that sometimes gets underestimated. Ideally, it's the beginning of a long and fruitful relationship between company and employee. Yet it doesn't always turn out that way, so to maximise your chances here are some key considerations as you enter a new chapter of your career.

First, be clear on your objectives and on the business context, and agree these with your manager. In his book 'The First 90 Days'[35], Michael Watkins describes four possible business situations and you should match your approach to the one that applies best:

- **Start-Up:** You need to move fast to build capabilities while learning on the job

- **Turnaround:** You also need to move fast to build on what works, but also change what doesn't

- **Realignment:** Change will be needed eventually, but you can take more time to consider your options

- **Sustaining Success:** Stay the course while you build an in-depth understanding of the business

Second, stay humble: Much as we all have a tendency to want to go in and do stuff, unless you're in full turnaround mode, I'd encourage you to spend the first month really understanding how your new company works, particularly on the cultural side.

Third, build a coalition and get some early wins. Think of it as being on a football team: you don't need to win every match but you do want to build relationships with your

---

35 See Further Reading for more details.

team-mates and you do need to score the occasional goal to show everyone what's possible in the future.

Fourth, ride out the 'valley of doubt': Most new joiners start in an excited, slightly euphoric mood given there's so much to discover. However, sooner or later information overload sets in, there are too many demands on your time and some things are not how you expected: this is the 'valley of doubt', where self-doubt creeps in and you wonder whether you've made the right decision. Accept that this is normal, keep the faith, start prioritising and come out happier the other side.

Finally, enjoy it. Life is full of excitement and while not everything will go right all of the time, it's all a lot easier if you remember to smile and see the positives. Take a leaf out of the book of Australian high jump champion Nicola Olyslagers, who before every jump puts on a big grin, slaps herself on the thighs and shouts to herself: "Come On![36]"

---

36 For an illustration, search 'Nicola Olyslagers World Athletics' and watch any of the top three video results

ACTION

Well done, you've made it to the end of the book! By now, you should have a long list of actions, some of which you've completed and others that you haven't. You might have also skipped some chapters in the interest of time.

I'd like you to find a way to continue the great work so you can keep progressing towards your goal. Can you try and schedule some actions for the future? Or remind yourself to come back to the book in a few weeks' time? Oh and tomorrow, treat yourself to a really nice speciality coffee or bubble tea or other fancy beverage. You've earnt it.

Epilogue: To moderate success, and beyond!

Imagine you're sat on sandy a beach on a Greek island. It's lunchtime, the sun is shining but it's not too hot because there's a gentle breeze. There aren't many people on this island, but you do spot a fisherman not far away, lounging on his boat. You approach him and after a few pleasantries, you ask why he's not out fishing, seeing as it's only early afternoon.

He says, "I've already been out once this morning", to which you reply, "yes but if you went again, surely you could catch more fish?" The man considers this for a moment and asks, "but why would I want that?" You're a bit puzzled but manage to reply, "well, to make more money, then maybe you can buy a bigger boat." The man once again thinks about this and once again replies, "but why would I want that?" At this point, you get a bit irritated and half snap, "well, so you can catch even more fish and maybe get a little fleet of boats". The man demurs and after a little while says for a third time, "but why would I want that?" You're getting quite exasperated at this perceived lack of common sense so you're almost shouting: "to make enough money so that eventually, you can just put your feet up and enjoy life"! At this point, the man looks you straight in the eye and calmly replies: "That's what I'm already doing today" before readjusting his hat and lying back down on his little boat.

This book isn't about lacking ambition. For a start, you're not spending your days on Greek beaches so having a bigger salary to do a few more fun things would probably be nice. And I'd personally get really bored sitting on that beach all day, so running a little fishing fleet sounds quite attractive. But it is about figuring out what success means for you and ultimately, finding a way to your own happiness. Which, weirdly enough, is way harder than it should be.

Given you've bought the book and you've made it as far as the epilogue (a heartfelt thank you on both counts), I'm assuming you do at least want to make it to the base camp of moderate success. And I know you will, although what I don't know is how long it'll take you to get there. Two years if all stars align? Or five? Or even ten?

At which point, the next big question will loom on the horizon: Now what? Are you happy with the views from base camp, or would you like to climb higher, perhaps even all the way to the summit?

It won't be an easy call because the higher you climb, the thinner the air gets and the more trade-offs there are — between work and family, between what's best for your team and what's best for the company, maybe even between your moral compass and the yearly bonus target — and it won't always be possible to resolve them to your satisfaction.

The good news is that those decisions can wait and by the time they arrive, you'll be older and wiser. For now, keep your eyes on the objective that you've laid out in the very first chapter of this book, and make it happen. I'm counting on you!

Acknowledgements

Writing a book is harder than you think, at least if you do it under your own steam, as I did. The first pass writing is straightforward enough (if you have the stamina): say you aim for 200 pages and you think you can write an average of five pages per day, then you'll need 40 days, so call it two months assuming an average working week.

But writing the original version isn't the half of it, because your original version won't be good enough. So you'll need to find an editor (or two) and write each chapter at least twice if not three times, based on their feedback. Later on, you'll want test readers giving you further feedback on the full draft.

And then the real fun starts, because a nice clean Word document is all well and good, but it isn't a book. You'll need a great title and a good looking cover and a spine and a blurb and a lovely internal layout, all the while picking the size of your book and the ISBN number and the publishing methods and the price and the weight and colour of the paper.

Then you finally have a book, but there's no point if no one knows it exists. So you need to switch your head into marketing mode and start thinking about LinkedIn posts and press releases and partnerships and podcasts and Facebook and YouTube and Instagram and a website and maybe even TikTok.

It's not just hard, it's really hard. And you won't get to the end without the support of a lot of people, to make all of the above actually happen but also to give you moral support when you think you'll never make it to the end.

I have to start by thanking my family. My wife Abi who kept reminding me that I'm temporarily an author so everything else is secondary, who put up with being interrupted ten times a day with yet another request for input, and who's been a blast to have around for the last 30 years. My kids Claudia and Tobi, who gave me honest feedback just when I needed it and made me feel like I was actually doing something useful. And our cat Milo for providing endless hours of entertainment and a reminder that life is good.

Thanks to the Wych Elm gang (Fiona, Jon, Matt and Sue), the earliest group to be subjected to my book related stories. Maybe their interest really was always real or perhaps they sometimes pretended, but it was great encouragement either way — and what a fun way to spend your Friday nights.

Fiona in particular claims that the idea for the title is hers, whether that's true I honestly can't remember, but who am I to doubt a lawyer: my heartfelt thanks, it survived a great number of challenges to emerge triumphant.

Once the project got properly underway, Amy Maxlhaieie was the first to jump on board and provided invaluable early advice on structure, particularly the idea to include an action in each chapter. Amy then patiently read each chapter not once but twice, ensuring that the stories flowed well and no mistakes remained.

Jen Fulford offered deep and thoughtful advice particularly on the more contentious elements of the book, despite having no time available to do so, and I really enjoyed our chat about life over a pint at the Olde Mitre.

Thank you also to my test readers Jordan Burnside, Vincent Cobee, Dave Currie, Sam Eads, Claudia Ercoli, Duncan Henry, Thomas Hlosta, Cat Muller, Riki Le Doze and Nishant Store. You all provided really helpful feedback, which I hope you might partly recognise in the final version.

Angela Freeth went above and beyond her role as test reader and then moved straight on to helping me with the marketing and sales aspects of the book. Her infectious enthusiasm (and willingness to spend her evenings and weekends on this book) were a great boost of energy just when I needed it.

Xavier Comas is responsible for both the fantastic cover design as well as the internal layout, and was always willing to answer my questions and do one more revision if needed. Ameesha Green gave helpful input on the early stages of the draft and taught me how to write a proper introduction and back cover blurb.

Daria Koren of Blackwood Group provided very thoughtful feedback on the chapter on headhunters (even if I didn't take all her comments on board). Do get in touch with Daria if you need to fill a role!

Thank you to anyone who engaged with my posts about the book on LinkedIn: I was blown away by the number of comments, likes, and reposts so you all made my day!

My other friends across the UK, the US, France, Austria and beyond who patiently listened to me blather on about this book of mine. I'm sure most of you thought it wasn't going to happen so thank you anyway, all feedback was gratefully received.

And finally, dear reader, thanks to you for buying this book (and reading this far)! It's what makes it all worthwhile.

Matthias Mahr, London, June 2025

Further reading

Good To Great: Why Some Companies Make the Leap... and Others Don't
by Jim Collins (2001)

On Grief and Grieving: Finding the Meaning of Grief Through the Five Stages of Loss
by Elizabeth Kubler-Ross and David Kessler (2005)

Transactional Analysis In Psychotherapy
by Eric Berne (1996)

The 7 Habits of Highly Effective People
by Steven Covey (2020 anniversary edition)

Getting to Yes with Yourself: And Other Worthy Opponents
by William Ury (2015)

The First 90 days
by Michael Watkins (2013)

About the author

Hi, I'm Matthias.

Born and raised in Vienna, Austria, I moved to the UK for undergrad studies in 1994 and since then have lived in Paris, Boston and London.

I have an MA from Cambridge University, an MBA from Harvard Business School, and spent 6 years in strategy consulting before moving into senior commercial roles. Highlights include starting the new London-Amsterdam service for Eurostar and more recently building Trainline's non-UK business by shuttling between Paris, Milan and Barcelona.

Now based in South-West London, I'm head chef for my wife Abi and my kids Claudia (17) and Tobi (14) while also trying to stay fit through orienteering, running and football refereeing – unless of course I'm off on yet another trip to somewhere new.

I truly hope that my book will help accelerate your career, or at least leave you with some thought-provoking ideas. Oh, and that you have a bit of fun along the way. Otherwise, what's the point?

Printed in Dunstable, United Kingdom